rebecoming

rebecoming

Come Out of Hiding to Live
as Your God-Given Essential Self

DR. MERRY C. LIN, PhD

BakerBooks

a division of Baker Publishing Group
Grand Rapids, Michigan

Published by Baker Books
a division of Baker Publishing Group
Grand Rapids, Michigan
BakerBooks.com

Printed in the United States of America

Library of Congress Cataloging-in-Publication Data
Names: Lin, Merry C., author.
Title: Rebecoming : come out of hiding to live as your God-given essential self / Dr. Merry C. Lin, PhD.
Description: Grand Rapids, Michigan : Baker Books, a division of Baker Publishing Group, [2024] | Includes bibliographical references.
Identifiers: LCCN 2024005419 | ISBN 9781540904102 (paper) | ISBN 9781540904201 (casebound) | ISBN 9781493445769 (ebook)
Subjects: LCSH: Self-actualization (Psychology)—Religious aspects—Christianity. | Maturation (Psychology)—Religious aspects—Christianity. | Self—Religious aspects—Christianity. | Spiritual life—Christianity.
Classification: LCC BV4598.2 .L54 2024 | DDC 248.4—dc23/eng/20240222
LC record available at https://lccn.loc.gov/2024005419

All names and details have been changed to protect the privacy of the individuals involved.

The author is represented by the literary agency of Pape Commons.

Cover design by Pete Garceau.

Baker Publishing Group publications use paper produced from sustainable forestry practices and postconsumer waste whenever possible.

24 25 26 27 28 29 30   7 6 5 4 3 2 1

Contents

Introduction

Embracing *everything*—from what I got right to what I got
wrong—invites the grace of wholeness.

Parker J. Palmer[1]

This wasn't the book I intended to write.

That could be why I procrastinated writing for two whole years,
and why there was such a long drought between this book and
the first one I published ten years ago. Sure, I was busy with life,
but now, looking back, I can see that the reasons I struggled with
this project have everything to do with what I'm writing about in
this book.

I first started thinking about the book I wanted to write on the
heels of the #MeToo and #ChurchToo movements. I was working
as a pastor in a church led by men. I experienced and witnessed
firsthand the pain of being female in a world that too often questioned the value of a woman's voice. And so, I thought I should
write to that experience and help women step into their full calling
in spite of systemic barriers. But somehow that message wasn't
enough to spur me forward.

Then, in March 2021, six Asian females were killed in a shooting
in Atlanta, Georgia, and there were suggestions the shooting was

linked to anti-Asian hatred. The uprising of hate toward Asians in the United States was exacerbated when the then–US president called COVID-19 the "China virus."[2] This violence triggered such a strong response in me that I was shocked at the level of emotional trauma I felt. But I didn't know why . . . at least not yet.

I only knew that the pain ran very deep for me as an Asian woman. Right down to what felt like my soul level. At the very place of my identity and worth.

Hearing about the Atlanta shooting forced me to begin uncovering and examining what had been buried deep in my psyche for so long. I don't think I could even begin to process all the layers of emotions I felt at that time. I only knew that I battled daily with insecurity, with trying to find my voice. I experienced a kaleidoscope of uncomfortable emotions like rage, fear, and grief as I faced the reality of sexism, misogyny, and racism.

I felt unanchored, like I couldn't find firm ground. I couldn't write because I didn't know fully what I wanted to say, let alone if I could say it. All I knew was that I wanted to scream, swear, and shout so that the world would finally pay attention. And listen.

But I wasn't sure where to go with it all, especially as a woman of color who has experienced racism and oppression and who has always coped by staying silent. Because *I was afraid*. Afraid to say the wrong thing and incite more anger and hatred. Afraid of losing the little remnant of "belonging" I had left.

In the 2019 movie *Parasite*, there is a poignant scene that bleakly captures some of the fallout of the Asian philosophy of fatalism. The director and cowriter of the film, Bong Joon Ho, hauntingly captured this philosophy when the father in the homeless shelter says to his son, "Do you want to know how you make a foolproof plan? Don't plan at all. Have no plan. . . . If you plan, something will always go wrong. That's life."[3] Watching that scene, especially after seeing the family's futile and darkly comedic attempts to better their station in life, stirred up profound sadness in me, and I could resonate with the character's underlying feelings of hopelessness.

According to this ethos, if we don't have dreams, then we won't be disappointed. If we don't have plans, we won't fail to achieve them. And since fatalism presumes that things won't change for the better—or change at all, for that matter—an attitude of resignation is part of how we cope. This resignation can lead to silence. We're silent as a way to handle the fear of disappointment, failure, or rejection.

Individuals in most traditional Asian cultures can often feel it's safest just to make the best of one's station in life and not "rock the boat" by trying to change things too much or challenge the status quo. Especially when white supremacy culture has told us for centuries that White people are better than any other people. For Asians adapting to life in Western cultures, our propensity to hide our emotions and present a socially acceptable public face has led to years of silent oppression.

I absorbed the message to stay quiet, work hard, stay out of trouble, and become the "model minority." And on the surface, life was good for me. Certainly, I am very thankful for the many opportunities afforded me in Canada that I might not have experienced had I grown up in Taiwan.

But I had never counted the cost of trying to fit in. I hadn't processed the impact of years of tolerating racism—always with an imperturbable smile. Always acting like it didn't bother me.

You must understand, I grew up in an era where there were very few Asians in my neighborhood, so I would often be the only person of Asian descent in my class. Bullying, teasing, mean comments, ostracism, and sexual harassment were all my norm. I can't even begin to count the number of men who wanted to have sex with me because they desired the so-called exotic experience of being with an Asian woman. These kinds of things happened so often that I became almost inured to it all.

And I coped by trying to fit in. By being nice. I learned to be a people pleaser, bending over backward to make people like me, with the hope that I could reverse the rejection and meanness I experienced just by being Asian. I learned to be extra careful in what I said and did, so that maybe, somehow, I'd be accepted. I also tried to suppress my Asian-ness when I was growing up, and I felt a lot of shame.

My history, like many of yours, has marked me with this feeling of "not-enoughness" as I tried to fit in as a person of color in White spaces. I felt like I didn't measure up, I wasn't good enough, and something was wrong with me. These feelings were only heightened and further complicated when people forgot that I was a person of color. When people assumed I was untouched by the racism occurring around me, when they talked to me as if I were a White person, I felt diminished somehow.

My own choice to act like I wasn't a person of color, born out of my longing to fit in, further made me lose sight of who I was. And when others also dismissed this part of me, the sense of not-enoughness could feel overwhelming. These tensions kept me stuck, and I struggled to find the message that fit my voice and experience.

● ● ●

Months passed after the Atlanta shooting before I could write a word. And even then, it wasn't until my agent encouraged me to write from the heart that it struck me. I had been trying to write out of a sense of duty, out of a performative place, in my role as a psychologist and "expert," and out of my shadow self, not from my heart or from my most authentic, truest self.

I had to go through the process of *unbecoming* all I thought I had to be—the nicest, smartest, kindest, Whitest person I believed I needed to be. I had to do some deep soul-searching, no matter how painful it was, to process my own story, its impact on me, and the strategies I'd developed over the years to cope and fit in. *I had to come out of hiding.*

I finally realized that this wasn't going to be a book about how to endure suffering from hard experiences like racism and sexism. This wasn't going to be a book about social justice and how we must change the ways in which we treat one another. Although these experiences and values are part of my story, as they may be part of yours, that wasn't the book emerging from the fires of my painful wrestling.

No, what was emerging was a book about how to come out from hiding—from all we thought we had to be to gain acceptance and love—and *rebecome* our God-given, essential self.

This is a book about personal transformation: mine and yours.

That space of in-between, when I couldn't write a word, was also a time of incredible personal growth. I wrestled with how to be my most authentic, God-given self, using all my gifts and abilities and passions for God, regardless of limitations. I had delayed writing because what was stirring in my heart was what I learned during this journey of coming out of hiding and during the deep work I went through in discovering what holds me back and why I self-sabotage.

While I continue to grow in understanding how my history, my gender, my race, and my trauma have shaped me, I can still thrive and find my truest, essential self within that reality.

Oh, don't get me wrong. It takes tremendous courage to face the darkness within us. I continue to feel—as I'm sure you do—all sorts of resistance, because it is hard work. The enemy within is often much worse than the enemy outside. But bringing light to the hidden darkness inside of us is the only way we can face the darkness outside of us with any level of integrity, humility, grace, and transparency. That's the only way we can choose better. The only way we can live as our true, essential self.

> **Bringing light to the hidden darkness inside of us is the only way we can face the darkness outside of us with any level of integrity, humility, grace, and transparency.**

Our Essential Self

But what does it mean to be our true, essential self? I believe that our essential self is our unique, personal identity that has been implanted by God in us to reflect his glory.

In the Genesis narrative of God creating and then breathing life into Adam and Eve, the biblical writer uses the Hebrew word *nephesh* to mean *life, soul*, or *self*. It is one of those ancient Hebrew terms that doesn't translate directly to English in a way that fully captures the writer's meaning. But in Israelite thinking, a person doesn't *have* a soul, they *are* a soul. It seems to indicate a human's personal identity.[4] Furthermore, in Genesis 1:26, when God said, "Let us make mankind in our image," the Hebrew word translated "image" refers to something that contains the *essence* of something else, in this case the essence of God.[5]

> Growth and healing aren't about finding more things to do, strive for, or achieve to earn our worth or our lovability.

And so, the thesis of this book is based upon the understanding that each of us is a soul, with an essential, personal identity, rooted in some aspect of how we reflect the essence of God. However, because people tend to understand "soul" in different ways, I've chosen mainly to use the term *essential self* to capture our God-imaging and God-given "soul-ish" self. You'll also see references to the *soul*, the *true self*, and the *authentic self* throughout the book, used interchangeably with *essential self*.

The transformation journey is about coming back to our original design, to the way God created us, to our most essential self, to the way we were meant to be and to live.

But—this is really key—transformation isn't just about becoming our essential self. It's about *unbecoming* all the things we believed we had to be to be loved. Growth and healing aren't about finding more things to do, strive for, or achieve to earn our worth or our lovability. If we turn growth into a to-do list, we will continue to live out of our protective *shadow self*, which is merely a broken reflection of who we truly are.

When we look to the external—what we do, what we accomplish, and the roles we play—to gain our sense of identity, we are living as our shadow self. We waste so much time and energy trying to figure out our "purpose," looking in all the wrong places, such as our roles, our education, our credentials, our reputation, and what others think about us. None of these are bad in and of themselves, but they become our idols, rooted in our shadow self, rather than an output of the fruit that comes out of a life lived from its true north: our essential self as created by God.

The good news is that our essential self—that beautiful, priceless, God-breathed part of us—can never be completely lost or destroyed or stolen. It may be hidden behind our protective strategies or what we have learned to believe about ourself to survive. But who we really are is always still there. We wait to be seen and invited out, for our pain to be healed, and for spaces where our self-protectiveness can be laid down.

Uncovering our essential self requires self-compassion for our stories of pain as well as tenderness for our hurting, scared, hiding self. It takes insight to see that fear, reactivity, and anger are our mind's and heart's way of telling us what we've been through. It takes courage to face our fears and soothe ourself in the face of our strong reactions, knowing that we are, after all, just being human. It takes perseverance to face the truth of how we fumble for our unhealthy and destructive coping mechanisms all the time. And it takes transparency to be vulnerable and to reach out for connection—the very thing we need to heal and transform and invite our essential self out of hiding.

That is the book you've now got in your hands.

From the Inside Out

Before we can begin our journey together, we must first acknowledge that what we know is different from what we *do*. And what we do is different from *who we are*. Many of us know what to do to improve our life, but we fail to move forward. We may know the steps to take to improve our life, but something within us sabotages us time and time again.

And that's because our successes and failures are rarely based on how much we know, our skills, or our expertise but rather are almost always rooted in the internal matters of our heart.

Dealing with these internal issues—our emotional needs, instincts, fears, insecurities, ego needs, triggers, motivations, and emotional maturity—will exponentially increase our effectiveness in life and lead to greater wholeness and happiness. The inner work we do leads to the outer fruit we produce. By switching our focus to this inner development rather than only focusing on our outer performance, we are guaranteed to produce the best fruit in our life.

And yes, wisdom is knowledge lived out. But wisdom itself is not transformation. For growth to occur, we must daily choose a different path, so that, over time, that new path becomes our norm. And as that path becomes our norm, it transforms who we are—or more accurately, it refines and brings out the true person we were created to be, rather than the shadow version we often show the world that keeps us stuck as a one-trick pony.

This transformation is a lifelong journey that requires a shift in our thinking, an immense amount of grace and humility, and great courage to keep diving in, again and again. Believing otherwise gets us in trouble, as our checklist form of learning—or, as I like to call it, our "tickity-box" activities—is shallow and doesn't allow our transformation to take root. The quick-fix mentality that dominates our impatient world can serve only to distract us from the lifelong journey toward wholeness.

I have come to learn—and I believe this passionately—that coming to know ourself is coming to know God more deeply. Let me explain before I am accused of blasphemy, because I am certainly not claiming we are God! I believe each one of us has been exquisitely made in God's image, but in a deeply personal way that is unique to us. We each get to shine a tiny, wonderful, sacred aspect of God to this world. Together, we form a tapestry of images that reflects God in a fuller way than we could on our own. So, as we know ourself and live out of our essential self more fully, we reflect God's glory in the way he has created us to do so, a way no one else can. And *that* is fulfilling the purpose he has for us.

However, truly fulfilling God's purposes for our life requires maturity. Maturity means we don't just show up without doing any inner work and automatically reflect God's glory. Yes, we invite Jesus into our life, and he does change us deeply, but that's just a first step. For the rest of our life, he continues to work in us so that we become more and more transformed into that unique aspect of his image we're created to reflect. As we work through all the internal barriers that hold us back and prevent the Holy Spirit from living through us, and as we welcome his refining through the painful work of inner growth, we are living in his will. We are living out our calling. It becomes much, much less about the goals we reach or the major initiatives we accomplish and more about *how* we live each day, in each interaction and in each relationship.

I've had the absolute joy of walking with fellow travelers who likewise have chosen to embrace the paradoxes of life, to remain humble and teachable, to lean into their hardships and pain to mine great beauty and refine gold and discover transformation. I invite you to come along with me as I tell some of our stories and share the lessons learned along the way. You can read this book all the way through as a pathway to a fuller life of health, freedom, and joy. Or you can read a chapter here and there as it speaks to you, to help you cope with something you're facing in your life. My hope is that you'll find wisdom from these chapters to help you along your way toward the grace of wholeness. I also hope you'll not just *know* but *do* the things needed to move toward personal transformation.

A Map for the Journey

I've organized this book to follow the pathway of personal growth: first, we pursue *insight*, which, lived out, leads to wisdom; and then *wisdom*, which, practiced intentionally and habitually, leads to long-term growth and ultimately to the fruit of *transformation*.

To lay the groundwork and help understand some of the underlying reasons for our common human struggles, we'll begin in section 1, "Insight—Why Do We Do What We Do?," with a brief overview of some of the basics of our human hardwiring. This section is key, as the rest of the book will make much more sense when you can see how your need for survival can save you but also entrap you. Don't worry; it won't be too science-y, and I will try to make it as interesting as possible. Worst-case scenario, you get to throw words like *amygdala* and *perseveration* around the dinner table.

Section 1 is all about gaining knowledge, insight, and self-awareness. That is a very important first step. Each chapter will address some of the ways you inadvertently sabotage yourself from finding true resilience, happiness, and purpose, and why you can be stuck in unhealthy patterns. It is the diagnostic section of the book, and each chapter provides an opportunity to see yourself in the stories and find insight and practical application.

By the way, you'll see that I intentionally include science, psychology, clinical experience, and faith all together in this book. I believe science is biblical, as it's rooted in truth and in how God has designed our body, mind, and heart. We can be practical and utilize what we are learning through science as we live out our faith in real time. Holistic transformation includes all aspects of our life: physical, emotional, relational, and spiritual. Living an integrated life ought to include wise and healthy choices in all areas.

In section 2, "Wisdom—How Can We Choose to Do Better?," the focus is on how to transform your knowledge into lived-out wisdom in a way that moves you away from your shadow self and closer to your essential self. Each chapter will help you be more self-aware and choose better, regardless of the forces around you that try to shut you down and the fears and insecurities that can hold you back.

Finally, section 3, "Transformation—How Do We Live as Our Essential Self?," provides a framework of aspirational hope to guide you in your journey of transformation. We'll look at key principles based on biblical truths and science (in how God has designed us) that are necessary for long-term change and transformation. Each chapter offers one of these principles, with practical strategies you can take to move beyond wisdom to ongoing transformation.

Each chapter also has a Digging Deeper section at the end that offers self-reflective questions to help you process through the content. Chapters can be reread to bring wisdom and hope to difficult situations. However, because the book is written to move you toward greater self-insight and transformation, if you read it linearly and "do the work," you'll gain a hopeful road map toward your own transformation and freedom.

By the way, you'll also see that many of the chapters suggest processing your self-reflection with a trusted small group of people. While this can feel scary in its vulnerability, connection with safe others is a key part of your transformation. So, before you begin the work in each Digging Deeper section, consider who could be part of your trusted circle. Even better, ask them to read this book with you and do the work as well, so you can journey together. In relationships where you experience authentic sharing, freedom to ask each other for help, certainty that you will stand in empathy and solidarity with each other, and willingness to provide honest feedback to each other, you will experience the freedom to come out of hiding.

Text a trusted friend (or two or three) right now and tell them you're going to work on your personal growth. Yes, right now, before you lose your nerve. Tell them about this book, ask them to join you, and schedule a lunch or get-together to talk about how you're going to incorporate this work into your life and how you can help each other and hold each other accountable. Call it your RB (rebecoming) group. If they're not willing or ready, or if they are taking too long to think about it, don't give up. Keep texting your friends until you find even one person willing to join you *right now*. Don't let the excuses of others become your excuse. You want people who will take initiative as well, so if they need constant reminders from you to even decide, let alone get committed to the process, they are the wrong people for you. Consider this a selection process and keep going until you have the right team for you!

Next, set up a group text or chat with your RB group. This will be the place you'll check in with each other, share your stories, ask for prayer, or whatever you need to stay on track. Expect lots of texting going back and forth on a regular basis.

Finally, arrange for a regular RB meeting with each other (monthly, bimonthly, or at whatever pace is reasonable and actionable for you). Ideally, try to meet in person, but if you can only do this on a video call, that's fine. During these meetings, take turns talking about your progress, your failures, even the times you forgot to do your home-work. Share about the insights you've gained about yourself, even if it's only something small. Every baby step is worth celebrating.

And for those of us who are Jesus followers (and I am unabash-edly, full-out one of those!), we get to join in with God's work of transformation in our life so that we can fulfill our destiny he has planned in advance for us:

> We have become his poetry, a re-created people that will fulfill the destiny he has given each of us, for we are joined to Jesus, the Anointed One. Even before we were born, God planned in advance our destiny and the good works we would do to fulfill it! (Eph. 2:10 TPT)

Come, join me in this journey toward becoming our truest, most essential self!

Insight

*Why Do We Do
What We Do?*

1

Our Stone Age Brains

I **felt completely gutted.** The rational part of my brain tried to talk me off the cliff, but its feeble whisper could not override the loud howling of my pain. I knew enough to walk outside and sit on the dock, mechanically putting my legs into the cool water, but I was unable to grasp a coherent thought other than the recurring one that I hurt. I hurt *a lot.*

One of my dearest friends had just said something incredibly hurtful to me. While the best part of me knew she didn't mean any harm by it—and was unaware of how racist her comment was—the primordial ache in my heart was too big to acknowledge that truth in the moment. I'd regarded her as one of my closest friends, but I now felt like she was my foe. Like she was against me. I felt about two inches tall, and in my immense pain, I blamed her for making me feel that way.

She had inadvertently triggered such a strong response in me because her words connected to my core feeling of not-enoughness rooted in my struggles to fit in as Other—a stranger in a strange land, an Asian trying to find my way in a community where I was always the different one. With one thoughtless comment, my friend triggered a cascade of emotions in me that were too big to put into words. They ran havoc through my body, setting off alarm bells. My heart was racing, and I felt an enormous pit in my stomach. Everything in me wanted to run away, to retreat. And, frankly, to break up with this friend and never ever see or talk to her again.

Does this story trigger any of your own feelings of not-enoughness, of feeling like an Other? Can you think of times in your life when you were hijacked by your strong emotional response, and the rational part of your mind knew it was an over-reaction? Did you beat yourself up for this very human response? I know I used to, and then the cycle would begin all over again. I would (1) Feel hurt or threatened; (2) React in an over-the-top way; (3) Feel shame and guilt for my overreaction; (4) Beat myself up; and (5) Repeat.

But I have good news: there's a hardwired reason for our dys-functional messiness, and we're kind of all in the same leaking boat. So, roll up your sleeves and read on. The concept is a bit academic, but I think it's important to understand so we can have compassion for our broken bits. Take a stance of curiosity, and remember: right now, we're gaining knowledge and insight.

Our Survival Instinct

As much as we'd like to think we've evolved since Adam and Eve first walked the earth, some things are just hardwired into our human physiology. This could be why we seem doomed to repeat history again and again, and why some of us take such comfort in reading the stories of all the human mess-ups in the Bible.

I've read plenty of history books, worked with many people from different backgrounds and cultures, and traveled to some pretty obscure places, and I have to tell you, we human beings have a lot more in common than we think. In fact, 99.9 percent of our DNA is exactly the same for all human beings![1] (I don't mean to frighten you, but our genes are 98.8 percent the same as chimpanzees; now *that* is worth sharing at the dinner table when your kids are acting like monkeys.[2])

So, while I celebrate how unique each of us is and have already mentioned how God has purposes for your life that only you can fulfill, I also want to emphasize how much we have in common with one another, regardless of our gender, race, sexuality, socioeconomic status, upbringing, or lived experiences. We can find compassion for ourself and others when we bond over our humanity. And when we understand our hardwired responses, *we can choose better.*

> **When we understand our hardwired responses, *we can choose better.***

Our ability to override our basic instincts and choose better is what differentiates us from our primate cousins. The more we understand how much our survival instincts drive us, the more we can be intentional about our responses to each other and to our environments. And be in control of ourself.

The human instinct to survive is our most powerful drive. It shapes how we think, what emotions we experience, and the ways we behave and interact with others. It forms what psychologists call *cognitive biases* that help us filter what our brain has decided is useful information and will help us survive and protect us from perceived danger. Given the millions of bits of data we are exposed to each day, cognitive biases help us process and remember information, problem solve, and make decisions. But of course, as the word *bias* suggests, they can also dictate what we pay attention to and why and how we react.

A pair of tiny, almond-shaped regions deep in our brain are central to our survival instincts.[3] These *amygdalae* (or *amygdala*, singular) are instrumental in our fight-or-flight responses and, in concert with other parts of the brain responsible for processing information, aid in regulating our emotions and encoding our memories. This, in turn, helps our brain figure out what's most important to remember so we can increase our chances of survival. That's why traumatic memories—even if no longer consciously remembered—can often trigger immediate and viscerally strong responses in our body.

And what are these responses? Depending on the situation, our temperaments, our experiences, and our interpretative filters, they include *fight, flight, freeze,* or *fawn.* These responses occur when hormones are released in our body, prompting us to stay and fight or to run and flee danger. The *fight* response is our body's way of facing perceived danger with aggression, either with our words or our fists, whereas *flight* is our body's way of avoiding danger by running away from the situation. In some situations when our body is completely overwhelmed and unable to react—either to move away or act against a threat—we might *freeze.* And in other situations, we may respond by *fawning,* which is to try to please someone to avoid their disapproval, anger, or rejection (a common response for those who've experienced childhood abuse).

While these responses can decrease our sense of danger and return our body to a calm, relaxed state in the short term, they might not be the best actions for us to take in the long term, particularly in today's world, where we rarely face physical danger. Because our brain doesn't differentiate between physical and psychological threats, many times we will respond in a reactive way when we feel threatened in our status or reputation, questioned about our abilities or ability to succeed, feel rejected by others, and so on. Our amygdalae responses can inadvertently harm ourself or others: our aggression can damage trust and relationships, our avoidance can cause problems or misunderstandings to escalate, our inaction can lead us to remain in toxic situations, and our fawning can give inappropriate power to others, even abusive others.

Our responses are even harder to track and control because of how quickly the amygdalae respond to perceived threats. We experience "hot" emotions such as disgust, anger, and fear instantaneously and powerfully—literally without thought. These emotions signal an imminent threat to our survival, which then initiates urgent action to increase our chances of survival.

In contrast, "cool" emotions such as joy, compassion, and love normally take longer to be felt and are usually less intense initially because there isn't a pressing need, survival-wise, to experience them strongly or right away. And guess what takes a back seat when our "hot" emotions are going haywire? With the cool emotions quieted, our amygdalae can hijack our brain, take control, and cause us to do untold damage to ourself or others through our impulsive words or actions. It's what we like to call our *lizard brain.*

Our perceptions and emotions that have survival value then produce behaviors that increase our chances of survival. *But* our survival instinct can also fail us and keep us stuck in habitual patterns of dysfunction and perseveration (repeating thoughts and actions over and over, long after the trigger has ended), especially if we're unaware of how deeply this instinct runs through all of our responses. It can lie to us and tell us we're in danger when we really aren't. It can move us to a stance of self-protection that blocks connection with others and prevents us from risking and growing. This instinct can be counterproductive and actively endanger our health and well-being.

How many of us have seen red and stomped away or yelled at someone, only to cause ourself more misery in the long run?

Another problem with the survival instinct is that it can be so subtle in how it controls us. For example, I'm pretty good at controlling my anger and fear and thinking (and, let's be honest, talking) my way through a situation. It's what I've been trained to do over years of deescalating heightened emotions and facilitating intense conflicts. But just the other day, I got into a bit of a tiff with my husband, and as I (calmly) told him all that he was doing wrong, I really hurt him. Now, I could have convinced myself that because I was calm and speaking rationally, I didn't do anything wrong. And my criticism was legit. But as I processed through why I said what I did, I realized that what had been triggered in me was the fear of abandonment, and I was trying to prevent that situation from occurring by criticizing him. It was all about *my* need for connection, not about helping him. Owning that truth will help me do better next time.

Clan-Living Hunter-Gatherers

Anthropologists and biblical historians are generally in agreement that human beings began life on earth as hunter-gatherers who congregated in clans. Evolutionary psychologists explain that the early conditions of earth created our basic instincts for survival, as they allowed us *homo sapiens* to be the all-conquering survivors. Now, we often think of instincts as something we're born with that are hard and fast and, therefore, immutable; however, science actually shows that instincts are not preprogrammed or simply genetically determined. Rather, they emerge each generation through a complex cascade of physical and biological influences.[4]

Similarly, creationists say that instincts are part of our original design, and God built into us the ability to adapt our instincts as we experience different conditions generationally, thereby allowing us to survive and thrive. All this is good news, because it means we can literally shape not just our own instinctive responses but those of generations to come!

There is an abundance of theories about our human instincts, with ongoing controversy and debate, but for the purposes of our discussion here, I'd like to use the popular Enneagram model of our basic instincts, as it fits very much with my own clinical experience.[5] This model says that our human instincts fall into three general categories—our needs to *survive*, *bond*, and *belong*—that appear to map onto different regions and systems of the brain that regulate our behavior, thoughts, and emotions. Honestly, don't you just love how God has created us and the intricacies of our design? The more I dig into science, the more I "dig" God, who is simply beyond comprehension in how beautifully he's designed us in all our complexity.

The first category is our instinct for *self-preservation*, which appears to map onto the ventral medial prefrontal cortex of our brain and helps create a self-referencing representation of ourself and evaluate potential threats and rewards.[6] This includes our need for food, safety, and shelter as well as much more complex needs such as our psychological sense of safety, our desire for health and well-being, and our desire for comfort and even pleasure. Whatever we ultimately believe we need for our safety and well-being.

Anthropologists explain that the second category of instinct—our need for *connection and intimacy* with another—is rooted in our need to procreate so that our species endures. Neurologically, there appears to be a link between this instinct and various neurotransmitter systems that modulate sexual desire, pleasure, and attachment.[7] This instinct drives us to procreate and then to create a family and raise our young to be strong and to survive. These patterns demonstrate how our Creator made us to be deeply known by him and by others. Regardless of the choice some humans may make to remain isolated due to fear, anger, or paranoia, left on their own they can never fully thrive. We have been designed to live in relationship with God, with each other, and, I would even say, in connection with God's creation.

Finally, humans instinctively create *social alliances*, the third category, because there is protection in large groups, and aligning with those who are in power and therefore have the greatest capacity to survive will also increase our chances of surviving. Well, wouldn't you know it, not only does our brain produce hormones that lead to prosocial behaviors but we also have mirror neuron systems that allow us to understand and imitate others' emotions and behaviors.[8] God has literally wired us to live in loving community, and we can do so much more to share his love to this world in community than we can on our own. We were never meant to live in isolation from each other.

The Power of Our Emotions

Today, many of us are trained to think we can dispense with our emotions in favor of rational analysis. But science tells us that emotions can never fully be suppressed. In fact, 100 percent of our human experience goes through the emotional part of our brain.[9] Yes, that's right. *One hundred percent.* We are always "feeling the feels," even if we don't acknowledge them. Our emotions are the first screening mechanism for all information received, and that information comes lightning fast, making it essential for our survival instinct.

All our decisions go through our emotional filters, so being unaware of our emotions gives them great power to control us in ways we don't even notice. That means, when it comes to our survival, our emotions will always come before our reason. As part of our survival instinct, here are just a few of our emotional filters.

1. *We give much greater weight and attention to negative information.*[10] Negative messages have far greater power than positive ones because our brain is wired to view negative—or "dangerous"—information as possible threats. When we feel threatened by negative information, stress hormones designed to prepare our body for fight or flight will flush through our brain and can impact our ability to receive any positive messages. If you have ever delivered bad news or negative feedback to someone, you probably had to navigate the emotional minefields carefully.

2. *We're really protective of our stuff—especially when threatened.*[11] If we barely have enough food and shelter to survive, we're going to be even more protective of the little we do have. After all, when you are living on the edge, to lose even a little would put your very existence in jeopardy. In wealthier communities, this emotional filter is expressed in how we prize our comfort and fight madly when it's threatened. Humans will do almost anything to avoid the pain of loss.

> **Reframing the status quo as threatening to our well-being helps us become risk-takers and engage in change.**

3. *We really don't like change and prefer the status quo, even if it's dysfunctional, over risky change with no guarantees of success.*[12] Although people are hardwired to act desperately when directly threatened, thinking outside the box and engaging in new endeavors are dangerous behaviors, and so we still tend to resist change. Any kind of change can feel risky when we are comfortable with the status quo. And yes, there are certain personalities that will actively pursue thrills, but most will stick with what's familiar because it feels safe compared with the possible danger of the unknown. That is why reframing the status quo as threatening to our well-being helps us become risk-takers and engage in change.

4. *We automatically classify others as friend or foe.*[13] To make sense of a complicated world, human beings developed remarkable capabilities to sort and classify information. As a result, we have become experts at making judicious alliances. Humans also have to know what untrustworthy individuals generally look like, because it would be foolish to deal with them. Thus we are predisposed to stereotype people based on very small pieces of evidence, mainly their looks and a few readily apparent behaviors. Personal experiences and culturally shaped mindsets further heighten our natural tendency to sort others into in-groups and out-groups.

5. *We barter information (i.e., gossip) and manage relationships for our benefit (i.e., manipulate).* Historically, human beings have survived by being socially savvy and knowing how to manage those in positions of power and influence who have the most resources to share. Those who know how to be political—who to befriend, what information to pass along—maneuver themselves to attain the right position with the right people to ensure their survival.

6. *We learn to be friendly and empathize with others to build peaceful social alliances.*[14] People are much more likely to appear trustworthy if they act in a friendly manner, and so can gain access to information that allows them to build alliances with those in power. Being able to guess what others are thinking and feeling allows us to respond in a way that helps other people open up to us. Human beings have become skilled at building peaceful alliances and pursuing win-win negotiations. People love to barter and trade, and it is through peaceful exchanges of information and favors that we build political alliances for social success.

7. *We gain status by beating our chests more loudly.*[15] To establish status in early human societies, people (especially males) frequently set up contests, such as games and battles, with clear winners and losers. Likewise, they displayed their status and mental gifts in elaborate public rituals and artistic displays. The purpose of such practices was to impress others and thus gain status. Today, high-status people (those with whatever traits are seen as desirable in a given culture, such as good looks, number of social media followers, or size of church congregation) are seen as having

a greater likelihood of "survival." As a result, many people spend oodles of time, money, and effort to increase their status, even at personal cost.

It can be seen as contrary to our odds of survival to be vulnerable about our weaknesses and appear "needy," as that can make us feel at risk of being hurt, harmed, or used. Often this type of false bravado can cover a deep sense of insecurity that can block us from growing in true confidence, which is based on who we are and not on how we perform (more on this in chapters 4 and 5).

We may wish human beings were more rational, but our brain, left to its own emotional devices, gets in the way. The truth is, today we need self-awareness, insight, and wisdom more than ever. The world is increasingly complex; we must make harder, more nuanced decisions faster and faster. And we must make those decisions while considering the impact on ourself, others, and the world. This is not to say that our emotions don't play an important role in how we make those decisions, but decisions based primarily on our survival responses and emotional reactivity may lead us astray.

Still with me? I know that as I was writing this section, I felt a bit exposed myself, but at the same time, I felt relief that there was a biological explanation for some of my behaviors that seem so irrational and hard to understand! I hope you're beginning to recognize that our shared human experiences can bring compassion and understanding toward ourself and others.

Let's keep going! In the next chapter we'll take a look at how our wiring is impacted by our experiences as well as the temperaments we're born with. Nature . . . meet nurture.

●　●　●　●　●　**DIGGING DEEPER** ●　●　●　●　●

1. Can you think of a recent time you felt hijacked by your strong emotional response? Did you fight, flee, freeze, or fawn?

2. Think about what might have triggered you. What was the primary emotion you felt? Shame? Anger? Fear?

3. If you feel able, talk to a trusted person who either experienced or observed your emotional response. If you can't talk to someone involved in the situation, process your experience with another trusted person who will be honest with you. The goal here isn't to beat yourself up but to recognize how your survival reaction may have impacted you.

Nature, Meet Nurture

The mid to late '70s was a time of rapid change in world history, especially with the economic upheavals following the end of the postwar economic boom. Social progressive values that began in the '60s, including the increasing economic liberty of women, continued to grow in prevalence. Second-wave feminism began to make its mark in Western cultures, and women were rising in politics and business.

Of course, I knew none of that. I was a prepubescent girl just trying to grow up. I was more concerned with how I would handle my recent perm disaster, spending frantic hours in front of the mirror with all sorts of hair products to minimize the frizz. I couldn't imagine there were greater crises that might be worthy of my attention.

I don't remember many details from that time in my life, but two conversations with my mother remain seared in my memory and still impact me today. The first conversation started innocently enough. I was curious and wanted to understand how my mom saw our family.

Yes, even then I showed a highly unusual curiosity about understanding people's psyches and motivations, all that inner world stuff I now speak about as a clinical psychologist. I'd like to think I was a normal child, but looking back, I think I was truly weird. Don't get me wrong: I have come to celebrate my unique wiring in how I process life, even in my early years, but I think my desire to understand and dig deep sometimes exposed me to things I didn't have the emotional maturity to handle, especially when my parents would forget I was still just a child.

My oldest brother had died just a year before—he was ten, I was eight. My parents never really spoke about the trauma of his death. I now know that it must have been a time of intense grief and turmoil. But all I remember is that my parents seemed to disappear, leaving eight-year-old me feeling alone and afraid.

We were a Taiwanese immigrant family trying to make our way in Canada and find that elusive "better life," and as an Asian family, talking about our emotions was not our way. We were also Christians who believed that God had his purposes for what he allowed in our lives. So, all my parents ever said to us was, "Your brother is in heaven now." End of discussion.

I remember my mom and I were in the kitchen—she was cooking dinner, and I was washing dishes. Another regular day in the immigrant life of the Chens. I asked her, "If you had to choose someone to die in your family, what is worse? Losing your husband or your child?" (I did mention I was weird, right?)

My mom paused, thought about it for a minute, and then replied, "Losing my husband. Because if you lose a child, you can always just have another one."

Her answer stunned me, and I remember feeling a mix of emotions. I was reassured because she had given me a "solution" if I ever lost a child, but I also felt . . . well . . . replaceable.

The second memorable conversation I had with my mom is one she initiated when I was around ten or eleven. By this time, our lives had become almost unbearably stressful. My dad's income was unstable and my sister's foray into rebellion had gone full throttle. As the youngest child, I knew from an early age that my job was to keep the peace and to help my mom manage the stresses of her life. I was not to cause any further trouble.

She regularly told me that I was her "best friend," and she poured out her heartaches and disappointments to me. She gossiped with me about her adult friends, and she seemed to take comfort in my quiet listening and sensitive responses.

She told me story after story, often repeating herself, of all the turmoil she had suffered as a young woman, having lost her mother at the age of sixteen and been forced by her father to quit school to take care of her younger siblings. She told me about her lost dreams of being a doctor, due to the misfortune of being born a female during a time and in a culture that subjugated her to a prescribed role.

She complained bitterly about the pain she was experiencing because of my father's poor decisions as the head of our family and the powerlessness she felt because of the traditions of our culture and our religion. I listened empathetically, because that was my role, unaware she was passing on the generational burden of shame, powerlessness, bitterness, and muteness that has marked the women of our family.

One day, while telling me about their decision to move to Canada, she shared that I had been an unplanned pregnancy. She then proceeded to explain how much angst the pregnancy caused her and how she had tried everything short of surgery to abort me.

It was almost like she was in a reverie, reliving that time in her life, and when she finally looked up and saw my face, she quickly reassured me that clearly God had plans for my life, because he didn't allow her to succeed in getting rid of her pregnancy.

But the damage was done. My ears buzzing, my stomach dropping, all I heard was that I was unwanted.

I grew up in an era when male children were far preferred over female children for Asian families. My family already had the incredible joy of having that male child as their firstborn. But then they lost him. All they had left were two girls. One was lost in rebellion, the other was unwanted.

I think my conception and birth story might have been re-deemed had I been born a boy like I was supposed to be. You know, the heir and the spare. When I was in utero, my grandmother—who was a very skilled midwife—had predicted that I would be a boy, based on my heartbeat. Right up until my delivery, she confidently said I was a boy. Even as I came out of the birth canal headfirst, I was chubby and bald, and so they began to celebrate that indeed this boy had been born, until, well, you know.

Looking back, I know that I was loved and wanted. I have happy memories of family time and recall instances when my parents demonstrated their love for me in practical ways. Usually through favorite foods, unexpected small toys I knew they couldn't afford, or the rare but coveted hugs. I am very thankful for all that my parents sacrificed to support me and to ensure I could achieve success in my life. I am especially grateful for their faithful prayers and the witness they bore to me as they lived out their faith.

But I know that the pain of those early years marked me. I know that shame, rejection, and fear have had a stronghold in my life because of these early experiences. I couldn't have articulated the impact at that time, but I can see, looking back, how my perfec-tionism, people-pleasing, and performance were born and took deep roots in the soil of those experiences.

I also know that my voice was silenced as a result. My thoughts, opinions, and actions became shaped by the fear of rejection. I alternated between shrilly expressing myself as a "strong" woman and retreating into awkward self-consciousness. Underlying it all was a deep insecurity that my voice even mattered, especially as a woman of color.

Many of you can feel my pain because it is yours too. You know what it's like to feel unwanted due to your gender, culture, or racial identity. Or maybe, up until now, you've been asleep to your own pain, but you are starting to realize that you've been in hiding.

And so, no matter how much you feel called by God to show up and speak up, no matter how confident you are in your compe-tency and capabilities, no matter how many degrees or credentials you have, a part of you hides. You stay quiet. You might say the expected thing, but it doesn't ring true. Or you fight for your place at the table, but you're always waiting for that shoe to drop and to be exposed or rejected. Kicked off the island.

Deep down, you feel unwanted.

I want to pause here for a moment—in this space of feeling our pain—and say that my heart is hurting for you and for me.

Writing this book has felt like creating sacred space for people like you and me, those of us who recognize we are hurting, long to feel accepted, and are courageous to face our pain so we can pursue healing and personal transformation. I just want to acknowledge that . . . and acknowledge *you*, and how very much you matter. And how very glad I am that you're coming on this journey with me.

Please honor your pain and your story, and pause at this place for as long as you need to before moving on. Close the book if you have to and go take a walk, take a hot bath, cuddle with your pet, or talk with a friend. Whatever you do, if you're feeling the pain of being unwanted, don't rush through it. Let yourself feel it, but also choose to take care of your heart.

What about Nature?

Before I talk about *nurture*, which is the main theme of this chapter, I want to make some further comments here about *nature* to wrap up what we talked about in chapter 1. Beyond the human wiring we all share, we each also have specific temperaments and genetic "imprints" we're born with, which impact our experiences and responses.

While our upbringing and early childhood experiences shape us (more about this in a minute), science shows that all babies are born with an innate temperament and have genetic predispositions to particular personality traits. Studies of twins separated at birth are the greatest evidence that there are some inborn traits in all of us, regardless of upbringing.[1] Current personality researchers have identified five factors impacting personality: openness, conscientiousness, extraversion, agreeableness, and neuroticism.[2] To make it easier to remember these traits, you can use the acronym OCEAN. All of us have aspects of these traits, but we tend to fall along a continuum of how much we demonstrate each trait. And the degree to which we have each trait isn't set; we can shift our position on the continuum depending on our experiences and growth. Don't worry too much about the details about this, as it can get pretty complicated (and not all researchers are in full agreement), but it's important to note that we do have inborn traits that can predispose us to certain responses.

I won't go into much more detail about these factors here, as there are many excellent resources available (just search "big five personality traits" to find these resources; there are also many personality tests that can help you identify yourself and the degree to which you display the various traits). But very briefly, *openness* describes how adventurous, curious, and creative we are; *conscientiousness* is how much we like to plan ahead, think about the impact of our decisions, and pursue goal-directed behaviors; *extraversion* is the degree to which we are energized and excited by being around others; *agreeableness* is how cooperative and trusting we can be; and *neuroticism* is characterized by the amount of emotionality and anxiety we experience.

Using myself as an example, I would say that I was born with the traits of being very open, above average in conscientiousness, moderate in extraversion, high in agreeableness, and (sadly) high in neuroticism. That means that as a child, I was sensitive, eager to please and perform to high expectations, and open to new ideas but quick to feel anxious and fearful if I felt unsafe or experienced disapproval or anger. You can see how I developed the strategies of people-pleasing, performance, and perfectionism!

Inborn traits also help explain why siblings raised in the same home environment with the same parents can have vastly different experiences, feelings, and beliefs and can use divergent coping strategies to help them survive. Yes, birth order, temperament, and experiences outside of the home can also shape us. But somehow, it is the combination of nature and nurture that seems to set us up to pursue unique, individual paths and responses.

The Profound Impact of Nurture

Regardless of how much our inborn nature impacts us, there is no doubt that *nurture* also plays a profound role in shaping our responses, interpretations, and experiences of life and relationships. Our early childhood experiences—especially our painful ones—gear us up to take on various stances of self-protection, which lead us to developing coping strategies that make us feel safe but can ultimately prevent us from dealing with the real issues or having our needs met.

As we noted in the previous chapter, God created us to be in relationship with himself and with others. God desires intimacy with us, and he's also given us other intimate relationships to help fill our heart and our longings for love and connection. When these relationships sour, our sense of well-being can sour as well; overwhelmed with hurt, rejection, and aloneness, we pull inward to protect our heart. Distancing starts to happen, and we begin to fill our emptiness with other things like work, entertainment, addictions, or other temporary satisfactions that soon become emptiness again.

> The interesting thing about relationships is that we interpret what happens and how others respond to us based on our early childhood experiences and the conclusions we made from them.

The interesting thing about relationships is that we interpret what happens and how others respond to us based on our early childhood experiences and the conclusions we made from them. The goal of understanding our past relationships isn't to blame our parents (many times, they really did the best they could with the tools they had) or to feel bitter over things we cannot change but rather to understand why we respond the way we do to our relationships *today*. Facing our past isn't about blaming our families but about taking control of our present and future.

39

Our ability to love and connect with others is based on our attachment to our primary caregivers. Picture babies being born: they are so vulnerable and unable to survive on their own; they must depend on others to care for them. And their experiences with their primary caregivers provide their basis for beginning to learn about themselves, others, God, and the world.

We all come into this world knowing absolutely nothing—a "blank slate." Our brains are hardwired to learn, and our neural pathways are ready to be established based on our experiences. These early experiences literally shape the chemical processes in the brain responsible for how we receive comfort, control our impulses, and calm our strong emotions.[3]

Research now shows that our brain's neural pathways are hardwired based on our attachment experiences. We are discovering more each day how dependent a child's developing brain is on the caregiver's sensitive, attuned, and responsive care—these early experiences literally shape the chemical processes in the brain responsible for how we control our impulses and calm our strong emotions. They form our *beliefs* about ourself, others, God, and the world.

> **How is our sense of our essential self impacted when we experience being forgotten, neglected, put aside, or made to feel not enough?**

How we respond determines our positive or negative self-image and our experience in relationships. These combined beliefs shape our expectations of future relationships and act as filters, coloring the way we see people and informing them (and us) about how we behave in relationships. This is called our *attachment style*, and how we behave governs how we attempt to control love and relationships (more about this in chapter 14).

Attachment injuries occur when, in times of stress, we expect a loved one to be there for us, and, for whatever reason, they aren't. Even those raised in caring homes have experienced various attachment injuries, from something as simple as getting lost, to experiencing a time of benign neglect as our parents struggled with other worries, to common disappointments when others weren't there for us.

When attachment injuries occur, the emotions of fear and shame aren't far behind. This is actually a good thing, because these emotions drive us toward connection. They help us reunite with our caregivers, get our needs met, and reestablish our sense of safety. And our expression of these emotions cues our loving caregivers that we are in need of soothing, and we need *them*. If such injuries occur occasionally, in the context of a loving home with connected, nurturing caregivers, we are not only able to recover but also learn to be resilient and recognize that human relationships aren't perfect but are *good enough*. We learn to recognize that hurt and pain are a part of human life and relationships, yet they don't take away from our essential sense of self and worth.

But what if these injuries are constant? Or traumatic? What if there is a consistent theme of neglect, criticism, or anger? What do these injuries do to our tender, nascent sense of self? How do they teach us the strategies we must take on to cope and survive? How is our sense of our essential self impacted when we experience being forgotten, neglected, put aside, or made to feel not enough?

Can you see how these repeated experiences can cause our walls to go up, and why our essential self goes into hiding?

• • • • • DIGGING DEEPER • • • • •

If you grew up in a home that was highly dysfunctional or even abusive, you may want to do this exercise with a trusted therapist. There may be traumas that are too difficult for you to process on your own. Even if you had a "happy" childhood, there will be experiences that were hurtful and even harmful. If you feel significant pain or want to shut down as you answer these questions, that may be a sign you need to reach out for help. Remember, stay safe during this journey, and don't do this alone!

1. When you think about your childhood memories, what themes stand out for you? Here are some examples of themes: *I had high expectations placed on me. Our family avoided conflict. It was sink or swim in my family. Competition and winning were prized in my family. I never felt like I fit in with my family; I felt stupid, smart, different, special. My family was loving, but there were expectations on what that love meant. My family didn't respect my boundaries. My home was very strict, and I was expected to follow all the rules. We were always busy and expected to keep busy. My parents gave me a lot of freedom growing up.*

2. How would you describe your primary caregivers? What were they like, and how did they praise you, punish you, or reward you? How did they show you love and affection? How did they respond when you "messed up"? How did they handle your emotions? Demonstrate their own?

3. Think about your early experiences outside of the home: at school, with friends, at church, and so forth. How may some of those experiences have shaped you?

4. Describe yourself as a little child. How would you describe your temperament? Picture some of your earliest memories: What were you doing? What did you most enjoy or hate doing? What labels were given to you by your family?

In the Grip of Fear

S tacey stared stonily at me for a few tense moments, her jaw clenched tightly and her pulse beating rapidly in her temple. I could see the muscles around her mouth working hard and her throat swallowing unconsciously as she fought to control her reactions to what I had just said.

And then she erupted.

I will not repeat the words that came out of her mouth as she shouted at me.

I let Stacey speak, even though every part of me wanted to shut her down. I know people sometimes think therapists are Spock-like in our ability to stay completely calm in the face of intense emotions and trauma, but trust me, it takes a lot of self-control and self-soothing to come out the other side of those sessions! My heart was racing from the verbal assault, but I knew we were on the cusp of a very important step for Stacey to gain self-insight.

I also knew that staying present with her in her anger and giving her empathy for her pain was exactly what she needed to get to that place of insight. My words had just triggered Stacey's very strong aversion to being vulnerable, and she was fighting hard to avoid admitting that her vitriol was covering up her intense fear of vulnerability and fear of the perceived risks if she were to let down her guard.

Stacey had come to see me because she was struggling with chronic insomnia, feeling on edge all the time, and having trouble dealing with the stressors in her life. She also acknowledged that she had gotten some feedback that her anger could be scary to her kids, and so she wanted to learn strategies to manage her anger better. She also wanted to work on her control issues, which she acknowledged were affecting some of her relationships, especially with her partner and colleagues.

What was making Stacey so angry with me was that I hadn't given her step-by-step strategies to control her emotions. Instead, I was poking at the possible root causes of her anger.

After Stacey wound down, I gently spoke to her and affirmed her love for her family and her respect for her colleagues. I acknowledged her longing to make sure they were protected and safe, and her desire to make sure her colleagues were supported to do their work properly. I also empathized with how empty she must feel, so close to burnout and unable to cope with much more stress in her life.

She looked at me with tears in her eyes, nodding as she heard me acknowledge her pain and her struggles. She then sat quietly for a moment, and I could see her fighting off her tender emotions of hurt, because those "softer" emotions only triggered her feelings of vulnerability even more. Before her guard could go up again, I spoke softly to her about how anger is often the way our soul communicates to us when we feel threatened, hurt, and exposed. And for some of us, when our survival instincts are triggered (that good ole lizard brain kicking in), we come out a-swingin'.

I wondered out loud if maybe she was worrying about her kids and her work, and that what she was truly feeling was fear; maybe her attempts to control them and the situation were her way of trying to prevent bad outcomes. I explained that fear is a primordial emotion built into every single one of us as a warning of danger (absolutely none of us are immune to fear, no matter how deep in denial we may be). But fear—in the face of *perceived* danger, rather than true danger—can cause us untold stress. Fear leads us to try to control the future so we can have a sense of predictability and preparation to face uncertain outcomes.

Stacey looked contemplative for a moment, then nodded briskly, got up, hugged me loosely with a rapid pat-pat on my back, and, without looking me in the eye, left the office. But she came back again and again to our sessions. I can't say she never got angry with me again, but there was a new understanding between us that allowed her to let down her guard and open up with me. Today, she is able to identify when fear is cropping up in her body, to override her survival instincts to go into fight-or-flight mode, to stay with the emotion of fear to understand what might be at the root of it, and to choose a better response that is much less damaging to herself and her relationships.

Our Nervous System's Response to Fear

Our nervous system has a natural rhythm that allows us to cope with the ups and downs of life. When we experience a distressing or threatening event, our body and mind go on alert. We experience *fear*. The body's alert system causes our heart rate to speed up and our breathing to become faster and shallower. Adrenaline floods our system. This amping up of our nervous system happens without thinking, and when we are in danger, it helps us run away or fight.

That is good news for us, as this wiring allows us to survive. But if the perceived threat and danger last for too long, our body may run on adrenaline for too long too—and then crash, leaving us feeling numb, depressed, and exhausted. While stress can be a healthy way to move us to action, the only good stress is *short-term* stress. Chronic stress, on the other hand, can lead to a myriad of physical and psychological symptoms that can have a long-term impact on our well-being.

And another problem with chronic stress? It leads to *chronic anxiety*, which is a constant state of unease in the face of imagined or anticipated threats. This can lead to emotional reactivity—which isn't good for us or our relationships.

When we keep thinking the stress is *outside* of us, being caused by others and circumstances, we feel perpetually powerless. Now, I'm not saying we don't undergo tremendously stressful situations or face dysfunctional behavior in others that impacts us greatly. What I am saying is there is a difference between what happens *out there* and what happens *in here*.

Stress is your *internal emotional response*, and that's what's causing you distress, not the stressor or the external situation. Stress is our body and mind's *response* to the external stressor. And it's the stress that harms you, not the stressor.

While stress can be a healthy way to move us to action, the only good stress is *short-term* stress.

Emotions, at their most basic level, involve the release of neurochemicals in the brain in response to some stimulus.[1] A situation happens, and your brain releases a bunch of chemicals that trigger a cascade of physiological changes in your body. Just about every system responds to the chemical and electrical cascade activated by the situational trigger. That's emotion. It's automatic and instantaneous. It happens everywhere, and it affects everything and everyone. And it's happening all the time.

When we experience stressors in our lives, we need to instruct our body that we're safe! We need to focus on what we *do* have control over, which is our internal responses to external realities. Otherwise, we'll stay in a state of stress, which can then become chronic.

Remember, it's your *behavioral response*, not the removal of the stressor, that tells your body you're safe. Your behavioral response can release calming, happy hormones and help you regulate your reactions—but you have to do something to signal to your body. Otherwise, it stays riled up. Your body needs the right body language to help you complete the stress cycle, which then tells your body that you're safe.

We'll talk more about how this state of stress can cause us to over-function (chapter 11) and how we can develop self-mastery to manage our stress response (chapter 13), but for now, it's important to face the truth that much of the time, what underlies our reactivity is *fear*, even if we don't consciously "feel" the emotion of fear. Fear of physical, emotional, or psychological danger. Fear of rejection. Fear of failure. Fear of losing control. You name it.

The Truth about Fear

Acknowledging your fears and facing them is hard work. You may be unaware of when you feel afraid, especially when you're used to suppressing your emotions and unaware of how fear can unconsciously drive you.

Or your fears may seem all-consuming and impossible to overcome. One of the major reasons people come into my office is to learn how to deal with their crippling worries and fears.

If this is you, and you feel like your anxiety has taken over your life, please get some professional help. The therapeutic strategies you'll learn really do work. So does dealing with some of the underlying trauma that could cause your body and emotions to go into "lockdown" mode, making it seem impossible to stop the cycle of fear in your body, thoughts, and emotions once triggered.

It is so vital for your freedom—for your journey of becoming your essential self—to face your fears, because the more you give in to them, the more fiercely they will control your life. In contrast, the more you confront your fears, the less power they have over your life. I have seen marriages, families, and teams crash and burn because of the stronghold of fear. Fear can become so debilitating that it will literally stop you in your tracks and prevent you from growing. I know this to be true, as anxiety and fear have negatively impacted my life, my relationships, and my faith journey.

Astoundingly, research shows that only 8 percent of what we fear has any basis in reality![2] Yet fear-based problems cause the vast majority of emotional issues. The amount of energy and time we spend on fear-based thinking is way out of proportion. We stay in a constant state of hypervigilance to prevent bad things from happening, but only 8 percent of our worries are legitimate concerns.

What makes fear even more amorphous is that it knows how to hide. Our fears can mask themselves so well that we are completely unaware of how they're controlling us. For me, I used to get defensive when someone was criticizing me (let's face it, I still do). I'd also try to control others or situations or keep busy to avoid facing problems. My favorite technique: eliminating anything in my life that felt unsafe or unpredictable so that I wouldn't even *feel* the emotion of fear.

> Our fears can mask themselves so well that we are completely unaware of how they're controlling us.

As a person of faith, the more I let fear rule my life, the more I moved away from God and weakened my ability to trust him. I could not grow in my relationship with God until I learned to deal with my fears. God commands us multiple times in Scripture, "Do not fear!" I don't think he is nagging us out of anger, disgust, or judgment but rather because he knows our human tendencies. He knows how fear will hide us from him and from our essential self.

Many people cry out to God, asking him to lift their pain and anxiety, but they struggle to do their part to exercise faith and confront their fear. Dealing with fear is not a passive exercise of simply waiting until God lifts our anxiety—it takes hard work, again and again and again. But I promise you, it gets easier. The burden our fears place on our life grows lighter the more we face our fears. I can feel the difference between when I am burdened by fear and when I have peace and lightness in my spirit. It is by daily, intentional working through of my fears that I can know this freedom.

Unfortunately, if we remain passive in the face of our fears and only commit "worry prayers"—repeating our worries over and over to God and spiritualizing the fact that we are actually ruminating and feeling afraid—we will continue to struggle with our anxieties. Ultimately, we will blame God and see him as harsh, abandoning us in our hour of need. But God knows that our life is never going to be struggle-free; experiencing fear, anger, and shame is part of being human. I think that is also part of what Jesus came to show us when he chose to come to us as fully human. He lived his life with "all the feels" (there are ample biblical passages that show Jesus was very human in his emotions), and yet he chose to face his fears, trust in his Father, and do the difficult thing. Character and faith grow by trusting God in the midst of our struggles.

Oh, and one other thing. I've also learned that at the root of my fear is my belief that I can control the outcome of my life. Yes, God gives us a lot of autonomy to make choices, and the need for agency is hardwired into our humanity. And he has also given us responsibility to choose better whenever we are confronted with our fears. But only he ultimately controls the outcomes.

Facing the truth of your fears is a very vital first step toward preventing fear from hijacking your life and your emotional well-being. It's important to stop denying fear. Stop calling it *prudence*, or *caution*, or *discernment*. And hang in there with me, because we are getting to the good news of how we can break free from fear!

DIGGING DEEPER

1. Think about how fear was handled in your family. Were you told to toughen up as a child? Did your parents tend to worry? Or did they simply "suck it up"?

2. When has fear prevented you from moving forward? Think of the people, situations, and challenges you've avoided because of fear.

3. What causes you the greatest worries in your life? Be as specific as possible. Is it your relationships? Your kids? Your health? Your finances? Your schooling? Your career? Your future?

4. How do you think fear has gone into hiding in your life? Do you overplan, try to control everything, or anticipate the worst-case scenario? If you're having trouble assessing yourself, ask a trusted person in your life to share some of their observations. Remember, if you're used to suppressing your emotions, you may not actually "feel" the emotion of fear, but trust me, it's there!

5. The next time you feel stressed, take note of what's happening in your body. Where are you feeling the stress? What is it in reaction to?

6. Try to think about your thinking. What are you ruminating about? What do you spend far too much time thinking about, instead of taking action? What repetitive thoughts occupy too much of your energy?

7. Think about the times you have felt angry and even lost control. What fears might have been triggered?

Shame on You!

Brandon smiled broadly as he greeted me, entering my office with his usual upbeat mood. He sprawled out on the couch and right away began telling me a funny story about an interaction he had with his boss that day. As we shared a laugh together, he picked up the stress ball from the coffee table and began squeezing it absentmindedly. Chatting casually, he maintained his usual eye contact during the course of our session but seemed to break away to glance around the room more often than usual. And while he seemed to be his typical jovial self, I noticed tension in the corners of his eyes and a small tremor in the muscles of his mouth as he smiled.

About three-quarters of the way through our session, Brandon paused. He adjusted his baseball hat farther down on his forehead and then looked at me with a half smile. "Um, there's something I wanted to ask you," he said.

With that half smile frozen on his face, he went on to share with me, for the first time, his struggles with pornography, asking me whether it was triggered by his current stress. He described feeling almost panicky, a sensation that was impossible to shake off until he was able to confess his sin to his priest.

As he spoke noncommittally about his experience, I could sense his pain, which perhaps went deeper than he was able to acknowledge. Because one of the areas we were working on was his ability to access his vulnerable emotions and stay present with them in a nonjudgmental way, I knew this was a pivotal moment in his journey of growth.

I leaned forward and spoke gently as I reassured him of how normal it was to be susceptible to unhealthy ways of coping when we're under stress. As I watched him swallow hard and wrestle to school his expression, I then spoke about something I called the *overanxious conscience*, which is the harsh inner voice that beats us up every time we mess up. It causes a loop of anxious feelings and compulsive actions in an attempt to ward off bad feelings and attain some relief.

And then I called his feeling what it was.

Shame.

I could see his growing awareness in his eyes as I talked about how shame attacks our very sense of worth, telling us we are bad in our core, and how often we try to manage that intensely uncomfortable feeling with our own efforts to "make up" for our perceived badness. Brandon was raised to believe that he needed to confess to be absolved of his sin, and he could not contain his anxiety until he could follow through with that act. But that confession always fell short, and it would not erase that ugly feeling of shame that kept knocking at the door of his hurting heart.

And then I spoke even more softly to Brandon. He sat very still as he listened to me, with a yearning in his expression I had never seen before. I could see his eyes glistening with unshed tears, and I knew his heart was finally opening to receive some much-needed truth.

I thanked him for his courage in being honest with me and for the privilege of hearing his story. I told him he'd just done an important thing to help himself come to terms with his brokenness and humanity so that he could do better. Not be perfect. But better. If he could understand what triggered shame for him, and how often the messages of shame lied to him and accused him of being worthless, inadequate, and not good enough, he could begin to see when shame held him back from facing what needed facing. He could stop hiding.

I could see the growing relief on his face as he shared his darkest and most shameful secret with me and saw there was no judgment. If anything, he watched me lean closer to him, and he experienced grace in the midst of his pain. Brandon had taken the first step in his healing by bringing his shame into the light and experiencing my acceptance and grace in the face of his human struggles.

The Science of Shame

We were created for joy. Can I repeat that for you? *We were created for joy.*

The Merriam-Webster dictionary defines *joy* as "the emotion evoked by well-being, success, or good fortune or by the prospect of possessing what one desires."[1] Other words that relate to that feeling of joy are *delight* and *bliss*. Don't you want more of that? It makes me feel all warm and squishy inside.

But hear me, because this next part is super important: *joy is the fruit of deeply connected relationships in which you are known and accepted.* Joy is the signature anthem of deep connection. It is what you experience deep in your soul when you're connected in a safe relationship. When you know you are loved and accepted. When you know you belong.

> **Joy is the fruit of deeply connected relationships in which you are known and accepted.**

Of all the important tasks of the developing infant, there is none more crucial than the pursuit and establishment of joyful, securely attached relationships. We develop our sense of self, efficacy, creativity, and resilience on that foundation. It is *the* thing.

A securely attached child is one who can explore their world with curiosity and make mistakes without fear. Their secure attachment to their primary caregivers provides the healing and repair of any distress or injury. Even in the face of temporarily unpleasant experiences, a baby's sense of curiosity and grounding in joy remain. From a secure attachment comes joy, and from joy comes human flourishing.

Without that presence of safety, rooted in a deep knowledge of being loved, little creativity can happen. Human potential can be cut off at its knees. The fear of abandonment is so rooted in our humanity that efforts to avoid the pain of perceived abandonment will subsume almost everything else. Shame is the state we experience when we fear abandonment—so crippling that it holds hostage our physical, emotional, and spiritual selves.

Shame primitively and powerfully undermines the process of joyful attachment, creativity, and flourishing. Shame is our system's way of warning us of impending abandonment. Because it's part of our instinct for survival, every single human being on the planet has experienced shame, whether they can name it or not.

Shame slithers its way into our stories at an early age. So early, in fact, that we usually have no conscious memory of our initial encounters with it. It can take place as early as age fifteen to eighteen months, and it usually involves a child's response to someone's nonverbal cues—a glance, a tone of voice, body language, gestures, or intensity of behavior—that interrupt whatever the child may be doing, delivering a subtle but undeniably felt message of disapproval.[2]

Shame is something that is sensed and felt in the body; a child often can't respond to shame with rational thoughts or words because their brain is not yet developed enough to make sense of what has happened. Shame is that hot flush of feeling coursing through our body—so familiar to all of us—that makes us feel flawed, inadequate, and never good enough. It makes us feel *yucky*. It's the fear of being unworthy of love and belonging, even as we crave those things to the very core of our being.

And shame moves us away from connection and belonging, which are the very things we need to heal our hurt and help us do better. According to shame research, shame is an intensely painful emotion that literally triggers the pain center in our brain.[3] As part of our survival mechanism, we will do almost anything to get away from that pain.

Some of us will *move away* by withdrawing, hiding, isolating, or keeping secrets. Some *move toward* by trying to please and appease, making up for our badness, or earning our way toward favor. And still others *move against* by attacking, using shame to fight shame, or trying to gain the upper hand over others, especially those who trigger our feelings of shame.

Any of this sound familiar?

We May Not Feel Shame but We Act "Shame-y"

There is something within the heart of every one of us that longs for acceptance, approval, and affirmation. We want to know that we matter, that we count, that we are valued beyond what we do for others.

But often from childhood, our tender little soul experiences hurtful experiences and wounding words that tear away at our sense of worth. We may feel lost and forgotten as our parents battle the stress and busyness of life. Too often, we get the message that we don't matter; our thoughts, opinions, and feelings don't matter; and being dependent on authority figures as a child means that they should decide what's best for us. And because our parents wanted us to "be good" and to succeed in life, they often inadvertently used shame to correct our behavior and shape our decisions. How often were we scolded for our mess-ups or warned sharply when our play or childish exploration led us beyond the prescribed lines of our parents' expectations for us?

When affirmation and attention are given to us, they are usually in response to our accomplishments, for being "good," or for our external appearance. We learn from an early age the importance of performance and personal effort in receiving the love and affirmation we want; we must fulfill our roles well if we want to be accepted. And so, we pour ourself into the different roles we play, while deep down we feel like we have no identity apart from what we do for others. We know that we're just one step away from messing up. Somehow, we don't make the cut. So we try harder, to avoid the painful feeling of . . . yup, shame. We act "shame-y," even if we repress our feelings of shame.

Lost in our secret fears and doubts—which we've all learned to cover up (often even from ourself), in case it leads to more rejection or judgment—we enter the adult world only to be assaulted by the messages of our performance-based and success-driven culture. Perfectionism is at an all-time high; we struggle to measure up to some invisible standard of acceptability in the world's eyes.

> **Shame is the "master emotion" that can stop us in our tracks.**

And if we're honest with ourself, we struggle with feeling like a failure, because we can't seem to keep up with everyone else. Or we literally work ourself ragged to maintain the pace, ending up with a host of physical, emotional, and relational problems we try to mask with medication, shopping, electronics, or other distractions.

Maybe most sadly, we don't retain any space in our lives to exist beyond what we do for others and the roles we play. We have no time to consider our identity apart from that. We're too busy, and in our mistaken belief that we have no choice and are doing what we're supposed to do, we do a disservice to what God is calling us to. We don't know who we are aside from our performance.

Shame is the "master emotion" that can stop us in our tracks. It can stop us from knowing who we really are, what we really long for, and what we're created to be and do. Shame causes us to go into hiding, pushes us to pretend, and forces us into a corner of survival and onto a prescribed path that we think will lead to acceptance and belonging. But instead, it leaves us shut out and shut down.

And in that isolation, we feel alone. We feel attacked. We feel misunderstood. And guess what happens when we feel that way?

Mistrust, broken relationships, and division. And yes, even ulti-mately destruction. Shame is at the root of many of the evils in this world, from abuse to oppression to injustice to war.

The Power of Naming It

If you've picked up this book and are reading these words right now, congratulations—you've already taken a first step to staring down shame and beginning to unravel the power of its toxicity in your life. Getting honest with your fears, insecurities, and broken bits opens the door to finding wholeness. It seems so counter-intuitive, when everything in your being is shouting at you to avoid shame and anything that triggers it at all costs. But shame loses its power to control you when you can face it with cour-age but also self-compassion. And as you begin to talk about it, you realize that you're not alone; other people struggle just like you. It is a universal aspect of our experiences that can bring us together.

Science now shows us that the basic neurophysiological pattern of shame is played out in large and small ways in our day-to-day life. But for many of us, and for much of our life, shame is far subtler and easily hides in the shadows, even as it drives much of our behaviors. These behaviors often unfold in micromoments—in both our nonverbal and verbal acts and our unconscious and con-scious choices. We cocreate barely noticeable schemas of shame that are woven into the fabric of our stories, our relationships, and our experiences.

While shame is often called the master emotion, you don't have to let it master you. You can develop *shame resilience* (more about this in section 3). If this chapter has triggered long-buried feel-ings, that's okay; in fact, it's good. If reading this has you going all Spock-like and feeling nothing, then chances are you're still resisting the truth. And that's okay too, but just try to acknowledge the possibility that shame may be controlling your thoughts and actions more than you realize. And keep going, dear reader; you can do this. We can do it together.

• • • • • DIGGING DEEPER • • • • • •

1. Think about a recent time you felt really "yucky" after messing up, feeling criticized, or getting negative feedback that really stung. If you can't identify with the emotion of shame yet, that's okay. I want you to think about how you felt in your body. Where did you experience tension? Where did you feel the heat?

2. How do you usually protect yourself, especially if you feel backed into a corner? Do you fight, flee, freeze, or fawn?

3. When you feel bad, angry, or sad, do you tend to move away, move toward, or move against? If you don't know the answer, ask people close to you and see if any themes emerge.

4. Over the next week or so, make a point to notice how shame shows up in your body, thoughts, and emotions. Pay attention to any "shame-y" actions you may take. Consider moments in your day when you felt tense, frustrated, or upset, and then think about whether shame was a part of your experience.

5

Behold, Our Shadow Self

I lived in a fantasy world of my own making. And I loved it.

Even as a young child, when other kids would go outside to play, I would spend hours alone in my room, playing with my Barbie doll. I could hear the muffled sounds of laughter and noise as kids played outside my window, but I didn't let them distract me. Instead, I would sit in my room and imagine all sorts of adventures for Barbie, making up stories about her exciting, glamorous life. With her, I could go anywhere, be anyone, and do anything. I could feel all her emotions as she embarked on her adventures. And I could imagine myself being Barbie—a beautiful, in-charge boss babe, free to do whatever she wanted. That was my secret life of play.

Now, looking back, I recognize that my world with Barbie was perhaps part of how I coped with the turmoil in my family: my older brother lay sick and dying in the hospital, and my parents were barely surviving and unable to attend to me. It might have been the way I soothed myself from facing the fears of the unknown. I had no sense of control over my real life, but I did in my stories.

Even when I would venture out to play with my sister, our play was filled with pretending, as we would take turns acting out different roles like teacher, mother, or secretary (yes, our world was very prescribed back in the '70s). Our imaginations created worlds of possibility; we could pretend anything into being.

We loved to experiment as well—like seeing what would happen if we bred our boy and girl hamsters. (What do you know, it worked! There were many, many hamster babies.) We tried to start a fire in our basement by rubbing two sticks together while "camping" under a blanket. (Believe it or not, we managed to make some sparks—a very exciting result!) We also loved putting on plays and shows, selling tickets around the neighborhood in hopes of funding food for the stray cat we found and hid in our garage.

I also loved to look into the windows of houses we drove past. I could "feel" the emotions emanating from those houses, and I would make up stories about the people inside them and the lives they lived. Depending on what I felt, their story would be sad, exciting, or dangerous. Funny, I never told anyone about this hobby of mine until just recently, to some close friends. I think I felt I was really weird even then, and so I hid myself.

When I went to school, I was initially a very shy and quiet child, but I quickly learned how to push myself to be energetic, engaged, and happy because it seemed to be what would make people like me. I did well in school, so I learned to study hard to achieve high marks. I learned by first grade to do public speeches, and I loved the attention I got. While I do realize that these skills have helped me considerably through the course of my life, I also know that the little girl in me—the truest essence of me—often went into hiding, and I would present the mask that afforded me acceptance. It was all about fitting in.

On top of that, being the only Asian person in my class made me work doubly hard to fit in. I took my innate sensitivity—my ability to read others and feel their emotions—and used it to shape myself into someone who would be liked.

Underneath the masks, can you glimpse the parts of me that were my birthright? My essential self?

I see my love of storytelling, my ability to listen attentively and feel awe at the gift of bearing witness to others' stories, my talent for sensing the emotions and needs of others, my deeply introspective nature, my love of fun and adventure, and my ability to inspire others with my words. But all too often, I used these gifts to shore up my shadow self, rooted in the motivation to be loved, rather than bravely pursuing opportunities to be my essential self without apology.

When We Learn to Hide

Because human babies have the longest period of dependency of all mammals, they are born with God-given defense systems to protect them from being too overwhelmed or harmed by psychological threats. Even in very dire circumstances, infants have an innate ability to survive because of these defense mechanisms. Over time, these early maneuvers evolve into coping strategies—patterns of thinking, feeling, and behaving. These patterns come to operate like organizing principles in our psyche that tell us how we must act to survive, which, in turn, become automatic habits and filters that influence where our attention goes and how we behave as we interact with others, the world, and even God.

Early experiments with infants demonstrate our basic human needs and the innate strategies babies employ to ensure those needs are met: for safety and security, connection and affection, and a sense of agency and control.[1] Crying is, of course, one of the most common mechanisms and can be used to communicate different needs. But children also learn to gurgle, point, or reach out for their caregivers—all in an attempt to achieve connection and ensure their needs are met.

One of my favorite experiments that illustrates how innate this is has to be the "Still Face Experiment" done in 1975 by Dr. Edward Tronick and colleagues (and since then has been replicated consistently).[2] In this experiment, infants showed distinct patterns of distress after three minutes of interacting with nonresponsive, expressionless mothers. While the focus of the experiment was primarily on the attachment between infants and their mothers, the results also show the distress infants feel when they lack a sense of agency, of being able to initiate and execute actions in the world to achieve a positive result.

When their normal strategies of pointing, smiling, and cooing don't result in Mom's attention, they become noticeably distressed. If ignored for too long, their central nervous system becomes so overwhelmed that they physically collapse, and then they withdraw and appear hopeless, no longer attempting to gain their mother's attention. Thankfully, the experiment also showed that the ability of Mom to respond and "repair" the relationship can quickly restore the child back to their happy, regulated self.

But think about this in the real world. Over time, a child may experience enough negative interactions to cause them to believe that their needs don't matter or won't be met by others. Or they may learn the if-then principle: *If I am "good," then my mom will be pleased with me. If I stay quiet, then I won't get into trouble.*

Eventually, we all experience rejection, hurt, mean words, or even abuse—all of which teaches our vulnerable essential self to go into hiding because it is not safe. To survive, we develop coping strategies to avoid Daddy's anger, to prevent Mommy's criticism, to stand up to a bully, to win a teacher's praise, or to achieve the approval of others.

As we develop these strategies, our shadow self comes into being. The shadow self looks very much like *us*—with many of the same behaviors, traits, and strengths—but adds a subversive twist that hides from ourself our true motivations for why we do what we do.

Under the Protective Cover of Our Shadow Self

I hope that, as you've been reading along with me, you've started to feel a sense of self-compassion and self-acceptance. Those masks you wear are there for a very good reason. Your shadow self came into being to *protect* you. Please let that sink into your soul for a moment.

And I want you to pause for another moment and consider this truth: authentic growth can only happen in the soil of grace. Anything less leads to the very traps of performance, perfectionism, and people-pleasing we're trying to escape. That's why grace and compassion toward yourself are absolutely essential as you face your darker side (more on this in the next chapter).

Remember, your shadow self is part of your humanity. It is not to be kicked to the curb. That is also why I use the term *shadow* self instead of *false* self, which has a negative connotation for me and makes me want to get rid of it, because who wants to be fake?

When your shadow self shows up, recognize that your sense of shame, fears, insecurities, or unmet needs have been triggered. And choose to pay attention to what has been stirred up. What unresolved pain, what broken bits of yourself are coming to the surface?

Our shadow self can do such a great job of mimicking our essential self—and protecting us from our fears, insecurities, and unmet needs—that most of us let it take over, to the point we don't even recognize it exists. Our shadow self uses our favored coping strategies to protect us and ensure that we achieve our goals, gain love and acceptance, maintain control over our life, and stay safe.

And what makes our shadow self so difficult to see is that these strategies work.

Until they don't.

Ultimately, these strategies prevent us from growing and developing the self-awareness we need to mature. They stop us from facing our fears and insecurities, and they prevent us from acknowledging our unmet needs, let alone pursuing healthy ways to get those needs met. And we literally become a shadow of ourself.

Our Blind Spots

While the term *personality* has often been used in popular culture as if it's an immutable part of us, more recent thinking in the field of psychology is a bit more complex. As I've said previously, there is evidence to support that we are born with some inherent

63

temperaments. But current thinking suggests that personality is more like the *personhood* we project outward, which can change depending on the context and our experiences. In fact, the latest research indicates that a great deal of our personality is quite fluid in adulthood.[3] Other terms that have sometimes been used in place of *personality* are the *idealized self* or the *ego self*. Regardless of the term we use, that projected self is born out of a combination of our temperament and our early childhood experiences. This self is *how we want others to see us*, and we will unconsciously fight to maintain that idealized sense of ourself, even in the face of consistent contradictory evidence. When our sense of self is so fragile that we resist facing the truth about ourself, we remain hidden and in bondage.

> Do you know what it's like being on the other side of *you*?

Yet our resistance to letting go of our idealized self is quite strong, to the point of self-blindness. And that is how we develop blind spots. While they may sound innocuous, those blind spots can be lethal to our growth and can stop us from rediscovering our essential self. In fact, a comprehensive study by Tasha Eurich and her team found that only 10 to 15 percent of study participants possessed true self-awareness.[4] While most people have some reasonable insight into their inner world, most were actually quite clueless about how others experienced them—what Tasha and her team call "external self-awareness."

Do you know what it's like being on the other side of *you*?

If you're like me, you've lived for years without realizing you've been hijacked by your shadow self. You talk yourself out of your pain and do whatever it takes to get up the next day and face your responsibilities. You might even pursue a passion for justice or help others exactly *because* you know what it's like to feel unwanted, to feel othered. Or maybe you've developed great people skills to help you connect with others, to pursue some semblance of feeling included, to satisfy a superficial sense of being wanted. And, secretly, you feel like you must always outgive, outperform, and outthink others, or else you'll be kicked off the island.

Does any of this sound familiar?

My friend, it's okay that your shadow self exists. It's there for a reason. The shadow self has its roots in pain, loss, trauma, and the thoughtless words spoken over you. And even today, your shadow self still shows up to protect you.

Don't let shame or denial shut your pain down. And face the truth that while your shadow self has shown up to protect you, it also hides the true essence of who you are, because the hurt has taught you that it's too dangerous for your essential self to be so exposed.

As much as I wish this weren't true, there is no shortcut to facing the pain of feeling unwanted or not good enough. The deep work we must do is part of the soul care we need, and it is the only way to declutter our heart from the debris that prevents us from experiencing, to the very depths of our toes, that we are loved and wanted.

• • • • • DIGGING DEEPER • • • • •

1. When you think about how you'd like others to see you, what words come to mind? Powerful and in control? Accommodating and a team player? Relational and caring? Creative and unique? Analytical and smart? Fun-loving and adventurous? Careful and detail-oriented? Driven and goal-oriented? Remember, your shadow self will have its roots in your essential self, so don't worry that those same qualities can also be part of your ego self-image.

2. Consider which of these motivations you most resonate with.[5] You want:

    To be strong and in control, and to avoid showing vulnerability.

    To maintain peace and be in harmony with the world.

    To be good and right, and to do the right thing.

    To be liked and appreciated, and to feel needed.

To be the best, and to be successful and admired.
To express your uniqueness and be authentic.
To know, to understand, and to gain knowledge.
To be safe and prepared.
To experience life to the fullest and avoid pain.

3. Now think about which of these fears you most resonate with that are most likely to lead to your self-protective behaviors. You fear:
    Being vulnerable.
    Being controlled and experiencing turmoil.
    Not being good enough.
    Not being loved.
    Being insignificant and useless.
    Being without identity.
    Being dependent/depleted.
    Being alone in a threatening world.
    Being limited and in pain.

4. Now, put your answers to numbers 2 and 3 together. For example, *I am motivated to take action/say things to ensure that I am liked because I am afraid of not being loved.* Consider what actions you typically take to achieve your motivation and protect yourself from your feared outcome.

5. Think about the last time you felt "yucky" after a situation. What was happening? What did you say? What did you do? How did you feel? In retrospect, what would you do or say differently? Try to separate your motivations from your actual behaviors and words. For example, I may be *consciously* motivated to help my husband by giving him advice (thinking it's for him), but my behavior can actually hurt him because of my *unconscious* motivation to feel understood by him (in truth, I'm motivated to protect myself or to meet my own needs).

6. Ask your RB group (or two or three trusted people, if you're doing this book on your own) to comment on what

it's like being on the other side of you. Let them know that you really want to know your blind spots, and ask them to help you identify those blind spots. Because you're talking about your *blind* spots, the feedback may take you by surprise, but try to remain open and keep your courage.

Wisdom

How Do We Choose to Do Better?

The Gift of
Self-Compassion

Nina nodded absently as I spoke, but I could tell she was not tracking with me. Instead, I could see her thoughts were looping over and over again as she ruminated about what she'd just told me about her latest dating disaster. Nina had just given me a small glance into her inner world, which was filled with self-recrimination and feelings of hopelessness that she could ever change.

She had come to me for advice on how to break her pattern of dysfunctional relationships with men. Nina recognized that the one consistent factor in all her failed relationships was *herself*, and she wanted help to pinpoint the cause so she could fix it. Fix herself.

Nina described herself as an overthinker. She knew that her fear of being rejected caused her to worry about moving forward in a relationship because of the possible disastrous outcomes. She also knew that she tended to notice the potential red flags in a person and fixate on them so that they became looming faults she could not ignore. And unfortunately, after each failed relationship, she would feel even more insecure and anxious about herself. She would beat herself up for the failure—and then rinse and repeat.

Interrupting me midsentence, Nina said, "I just can't seem to stop attracting these losers! What is it about me that keeps finding these guys who don't want to commit, and so I keep getting hurt?"

"Nina," I began, but she didn't appear to hear me. She continued to talk even more harshly about herself, her voice rising as tears began to course down her cheeks. I could see that she was lost in her own world of insecurity and self-blame, and her inner critic had her firmly in its grip.

I repeated her name, loudly. She finally stopped and looked at me.

"Nina," I said again, more gently. "I can see you're in so much pain. It's tough when you long so much for a partner and yet you're still alone, no matter how hard you try. I can't even begin to imagine how painful this must be for you. My heart is aching for you right now."

Nina broke down at this point and began sobbing. With her permission, I reached over and stroked her arm softly while she cried. I knew she was grieving the possible loss of her dream for a life partner, and I could sense her deep loneliness as she contemplated life on her own. But worse, I could sense her hopelessness, which was causing her to spiral into a dark place.

After her weeping quieted down, I said, "Nina, it hurts me to hear you talk about yourself so harshly. I know you would never say those things to a friend, yet somehow you speak about yourself with such self-criticism."

She looked up at me, surprised. This was the first time I had spoken so directly to her and shared how her habitual pattern of self-blame was hard for me to witness. I could see that she was finally paying close attention to my words.

I talked with her about how her inner critic was keeping her stuck in a place of hopelessness because it was pushing her to unrealistic standards and constant self-recrimination. I reminded her that true growth only happens in the soil of grace, when we actually believe in our ability to change and do better. In this place of compassion and understanding, we are much more likely to have a growth mindset and be able to summon the grit and persistence required to change our dysfunctional patterns.

Nina became more attentive as I spoke. My compassion and care for her had finally broken through her negative spiraling. Her heart was now ready to hear the truth about how her harsh inner critic was keeping her stuck. She was able to recognize *this* was the pattern that was most damaging to her and her ability to achieve her dream for a life partner.

Having grown up with demanding parents, Nina had internalized their unrealistic standards for her, and she had unknowingly taken on their harsh judgments whenever she felt she failed to meet her own expectations. As a child, whenever she met with parental criticism, she would feel deflated and hopeless, like there was nothing she could ever do to please them. As an adult, she came to see that they truly believed they were helping her be her very best, and she understood their underlying motivations—but she'd neglected to examine the impact these experiences and patterns had on her.

The Need for Self-Compassion

Dr. Kristin Neff, a pioneer in the field of self-compassion research, has published study after study demonstrating the power of self-compassion to help growth in resilience, improve performance, reduce psychological distress, overcome trauma, enhance effectiveness as a parent, experience more happiness in romantic relationships, and increase mental and physical well-being.[1] Self-compassion motivates us to make healthy changes and gives us a sense of belief in ourself and patience for the process of growth. It moves us *toward* self-improvement, whereas self-criticism moves us *away* from personal growth.

Dr. Neff describes self-compassion this way:

> [It is] compassion for the experience of suffering turned inward . . . [and] how we relate to ourselves in instances of perceived failure,

inadequacy, or personal suffering. . . . This feeling is warm and caring rather than cold and judgmental, wanting to help rather than harm. . . . It involves being present with our own pain, feeling connected to others who are also suffering, and understanding and supporting ourselves through difficult moments.[2]

Self-compassion involves an acceptance of our humanity and brokenness rather than judgment. It means being kind to ourself, much like we would be to a hurting friend, showing empathy for our distress, and responding to ourself with warmth and care. It also means actively pursuing activities of self-care and self-soothing (which help our amygdalae calm down and prevent our lizard brain from sabotaging us), so that we can be in a much better place to problem solve and take steps to learn from our mistakes and change direction.

When we ignore or denigrate our pain, we can become so absorbed by our negative reactions and thoughts that we can't step outside of ourself and care well for our soul.[3] This kind of rumination highlights all our shortcomings and damages our sense of worth, pushing our essential self into further hiding. Overidentification with our failures feels more like a permanent part of ourself rather than an aspect we can change, and we begin to see ourself *as* a failure instead of someone who has failed.

The Power of Self-Compassion

Contrary to what some may think, self-compassion does *not* mean hiding from the truth of our limitations and weaknesses. Rather it allows us to face our need for growth with a sense of hope and helps us foster more realistic self-appraisal.

We don't need to hide behind our puffed-up shadow self and avoid our insecurities and fears. Instead of fearing our inadequacies, we are motivated by self-compassion to improve, as it's rooted in our God-given desire to be our best self. Instead of harsh criticism, self-compassion utilizes encouragement and constructive feedback. Instead of blame and denial, self-compassion allows us to take personal responsibility for our actions. And instead of a focus on performance, self-compassion is about *mastery*, which is an intrinsic desire to learn and grow and an ability to see failure as an opportunity to learn.[4]

Self-compassion is not the same thing as self-esteem. Instead, having self-compassion means we acknowledge with kindness our shared and imperfect human condition. In fact, research shows that self-compassion is associated with a more stable sense of self that doesn't rely on appearance, performance, or social approval— all the things our shadow self depends on for a sense of worth. Studies also show that self-compassion enhances our ability to care well for others by improving our connections with them, leading to greater perspective taking, forgiveness of others, and acceptance of them and their flaws. In contrast, studies also reveal that while self-esteem can build our sense of self, it can also increase our narcissism, our judgment of others, our feelings of superiority to others, and our need to defend our own viewpoints.[5]

Common Humanity

Most importantly, self-compassion allows us to recognize that life struggles are common to all of humanity, and it helps us to move toward connection with others rather than stay isolated in our pain (more about this in chapter 14). The word *compassion* in its Latin root literally means "to suffer with." Built within the gift of compassion is a sense of being with others in our common suffering, rather than being alone. Simply knowing we are not alone in our suffering gives us greater resilience to fight our dragons. It helps us to do better.

Just search the word *compassion* in the Bible, and you will see verse after verse reminding us of God's mercy and compassion for us. He stooped down and became like us—he became human and suffered in his humanity to show us how he identified with our suffering, how he suffered with and for us, and how much he loves all of us broken, hurting, imperfect humans. Jesus demonstrated his solidarity with our humanity so that we could not only understand the depth and breadth of his love for us but also offer that same compassion and love to ourself and others.

Our inner critic lies to us and tells us that no one is as bad as we are, that somehow we're the only one who's blowing it big-time. It distorts reality so that we feel like only we deserve such punishment. Can you see how this would keep us stuck? This is the root of why many of us deny our need to grow, refuse to ask for help, or feel helpless to make any changes in our life.

It is a common misbelief to think that self-criticism will help us improve or that guilt will somehow motivate us to change. And it can give us a false sense of control. We tell ourself, *If I criticize myself first, I can avoid the pain of being criticized by others.* Unfortunately, criticism is much more likely to provoke anxiety and shame rather than hope. It can trigger our survival response, which can lead to heightened amygdalae responses and make us more likely to go into fight, flight, freeze, or fawn mode. Which only keeps us hiding in our shadow self, isolated and unable to show up as our essential self for fear of being rejected.

The good news is that self-compassion is a skill that can be learned and practiced. But it does require the courage to open ourself up to others first, as *experiencing* compassion from others is a necessary step to recognizing that feeling of warmth, understanding, and care. The more we experience soothing and comfort from others, the more we can internalize those good feelings and begin to produce them for ourself. When infants experience the nurturing love of their caregivers, they eventually internalize that feeling so it becomes part of their neural pathways and a recognizable response to when they feel pain and need comfort.

For those of us who unfortunately did not experience that kind of nurturing from our caregivers, it's never too late! Whether with a therapist, pastor, or coach, we can learn to accept compassion from others so that we can begin to give that much-needed resource to ourself. While we can experience this kind of care from our friends and family, our inner critic may not be able to receive compassion from our loved ones as readily as from a more removed figure. We tend to question their motivations more, we may not want to burden them with our problems, or we may tend to be attracted to family relationships that are less healthy and repeat our early family dysfunction.

Psychotherapy is designed to help clients take a less judgmental and kinder approach to their suffering, to become more aware of their own needs, to care for their own well-being, and to tolerate distress. Studies show that sessions with a competent psychotherapist, regardless of their therapeutic orientation, increase a person's self-compassion, which also leads to a stable decrease in their mental health symptoms.[6]

Aside from pursuing psychotherapy, you can incorporate simple practices into your daily routine that can help you develop your capacity for self-compassion. For example, Dr. Neff offers some guided self-compassion practices and exercises on her website that are worth trying.[7] You can also explore faith-based exercises (see below) that help you to practice self-compassion in the presence of the One who loves you more than life itself.

If you're beginning to recognize your need for self-compassion, my heart is filled to overflowing with such hope for you! Know that my heart is reaching out through these pages to extend you compassion, acceptance, and empathy as you embark on this journey toward rebecoming.

DIGGING DEEPER

1. Awareness is the first step to recognizing and letting go of your inner critic. Think about the last time you beat yourself up for a mistake you made. What happened? What were you feeling? How did you respond?

2. Try keeping track of how often your inner critic shows up. What are some of the phrases your inner critic likes to use? For example, *You're so stupid. You're such a loser! Why are you such a mess? How could you do this to your child/friend/partner?* How do you feel as you hear those

phrases in your head? What are you afraid of feeling (perhaps some of your vulnerable feelings of grief and unmet longings)?

3. What are some opposite truths you can use to combat the lies of your inner critic? If this is hard for you, consider what you would say to a beloved friend who was saying these negative phrases to themself. Try expressing empathy toward yourself as you would toward a friend.

4. Incorporate receiving compassion from God into your quiet time practice. Start with your hands down in your lap and begin to tell him all that is on your mind and all your feelings. Don't hold back! If you journal, write all your thoughts and feelings to God instead. Then take a few deep, cleansing breaths, counting in 4-6-8 (breathe in through your nose for 4 beats, hold for 6 beats, then breathe out through your mouth for 8 beats). You may find it helpful to incorporate phrases of 4-6-8 syllables to say in your head rather than counting, such as *Jesus loves me* (4), *My Father is with me* (6), and *I am a beloved child of God* (8). Next, hold your hands palm-upward and open on your lap, and say or write to God, "My heart is open to hearing from you and receiving your love." Then ask him, "What is on your heart for me today?"

Don't worry if you don't immediately hear or sense anything. This practice is more about getting into a posture of receiving from God and stilling yourself long enough to experience his love for you. Over time, you will begin to sense his love for you. When you're raw and honest with God (don't be afraid to be angry and say whatever you need to say), he still responds with such kindness and compassion.

If what you sense seems angry, harsh, or punitive, then it is *not* from God, and you can respond with something like, "I reject those lies, in Jesus's name." Continue to pray and ask to hear from the true Lord Jesus. Consider also asking him to show you signs of his love and compassion throughout the day, and then intentionally look for them. This spiritual practice will also help you rewire your brain to notice and focus on love, compassion, and grace rather than criticism, self-hatred, and shame.

Trust Issues

Jared slouched back on the couch with his arms crossed and his baseball hat tipped low over his forehead, shielding his eyes from my gaze. Everything about his body language screamed, *Keep out!* He muttered monosyllabic responses to every one of my questions, and then right in the middle of our session, he took out his cell phone and began to scroll.

Jared had been referred to me by his employer for "leadership coaching" (read, *anger management*) because he had been systematically alienating his team members with biting comments, harsh criticisms, demanding directives, and a controlling style of leadership. He had risen very quickly in the organization as a young talent due to his ability to achieve aggressive goals, his incisive decision-making, his persuasive abilities, and his brilliant mind. But he was also known to be a loner who preferred autonomy and the freedom to run projects as he saw fit. While Jared seemed to attract admirers of his charismatic personality (and let's be honest, his abilities as a rainmaker), he rarely socialized with his colleagues.

None of his habits had seemed to be an issue until Jared had risen in the organization and left behind him a slew of employees quitting, changing to different departments, or lodging complaints with HR. When his boss tried to talk to him about this pattern, Jared alternated between aggressively defending himself and acting like he felt he was a victim of persecution. Nothing worked to change Jared's behavior. Hence, him sitting in my office, clearly angry and resistant to being there.

I decided to take the bull by the horns and said to Jared, "I know you don't want to be here, and you probably feel like this is a waste of your time."

He looked up, momentarily surprised, before glancing back down at his phone.

I went on to say, "I don't blame you for feeling this way. I'd feel the same way if my boss made me go for coaching. And frankly, we *are* wasting your time, because coaching is never helpful unless someone actually chooses to be here."

I finally had his attention.

"So, you have a choice: we can sit here while you scroll on your phone and just go through the motions, or we can use this time—that's paid for anyway—to talk about whatever you want. I can tell you this: I'm not here to change you, correct you, or criticize you. I've been hired as *your* coach, which means I'm *for* you."

Jared looked skeptical, but he also seemed to become less wary. I went on to explain to him about confidentiality, that I had his boss's agreement that nothing we talked about in our sessions would be shared with her unless Jared wanted it shared. Nor would I be giving her any updates on his "progress" or getting input from her about his work performance, again unless he wanted it. I'd intentionally set up our process this way, knowing I had to build trust with Jared before there was even a chance of making any headway with him.

It took several more sessions, but Jared eventually opened up and shared some of his history with me. He grew up as an only child to immigrant parents, and expectations were high. He had a demanding mom who was often angry and critical of him and a dad who was emotionally disengaged, likely suffered from depression, and spent all his time at home hiding in his workshop. On top of that, Jared struggled in school with dyslexia, and so endured years of bullying and teasing from his peers until he grew big enough to fight back. He also found his niche by excelling at sports, where he was often sought for his top-notch skills, and eventually he won a sports scholarship to a prestigious university. He'd taken his ability to win to the corporate world and hadn't looked back since.

But deep down, Jared had been struggling with burnout, driven by an unrelenting pressure to succeed. He started to acknowledge feelings of depression, anxiety, and loneliness. It wasn't easy for him, but as I showed consistent compassion and empathy, he finally began to let down his guard and to trust me. He started seeing how his patterns of self-protectiveness, wariness, and fear of being vulnerable with others were really a manifestation of all the trauma he had experienced growing up, and the sense that he had no choice but to defend and take care of himself because no one else would do it for him. He began to gain insight into how his self-protective behaviors were pushing others away and impacting his effectiveness as a leader.

At his lowest point, when he felt the most vulnerable, Jared finally experienced a breakthrough and began to grieve and process his trauma. It was only then that he was able to turn his growing self-insight into actionable changes in his behavior and interactions with others. This progress didn't happen because I took him through a series on leadership training or taught him strategies to lead others well. Rather, his growth occurred because he experienced healing that moved him from his self-protective stance to genuinely wanting to change and grow as a person and as a leader.

The Frozen Heart Syndrome

In the 2013 Disney movie *Frozen*, one of the main characters, Elsa, has the power to turn everything and everyone into ice if she touches them. Because this power can cause harm to others, she chooses to protect her loved ones by withdrawing completely to a solitary and cold mountaintop, where she intends to live on her own for the rest of her life.

One of the most compelling scenes for me is when Elsa is on the mountain and singing about how she can be herself without fear, that she'll be just fine on her own, that she doesn't need anyone—that she's finally free. But there's also deep sadness to her story because she thinks she has to be alone forever. She may be "safe," but she can never experience love and relationship.

Do you know what underlies her decision to be alone?

Fear.

In the real world, fear is often what underlies problems in relationships. It's often why we withdraw, and it's also why we attack in anger and push people away. We want to protect ourself from pain. We're afraid of rejection, abandonment, and hurt. But this fear is the core of our trust issues. Our fear of pain and our inability to trust causes us to shut down from the very relationships we need to heal.

Some of the angriest people we know are lonely, but they can't face the pain of their aloneness, so they keep their hearts hard and push others away with their anger—they keep their hearts frozen. But some of the most loving and caring people are also lonely (this was *me* at one point in my life). We fill our time nurturing others, but when it comes to our own emotional needs and pain, we bury our heart. We, too, have a frozen heart because we never expose our own emotional vulnerabilities—we've shut down our needs to focus completely on others. That way we can guarantee people will remain in our life, that they will always need, use, and "love" us for what we do for them. It feels safer, right?

> **Freedom isn't in solitude or withdrawal but in *love*, which has the power to heal and save.**

I call this the *frozen heart syndrome*, not because we're cold or calculating but because we've shut down our heart to protect ourself. *If I don't feel, I won't hurt. If I don't love, I won't lose. If I'm not vulnerable, I won't be rejected.* But that isn't the way God has wired us to live. We are created for mutual and intimate relationships and connection to God our Father and each other.

The moral at the end of *Frozen* is that freedom isn't in solitude or withdrawal but in *love*, which has the power to heal and save—something we may need to reteach ourself.

Stuck in Our Past

If you've never taken the time to examine how your past experiences and upbringing affect you, I can guarantee you they are impacting your life today—and likely not for the best. Beyond examining your relationship to your past, how aware are you of your "hot spots"—the people and experiences that trigger strong, negative emotions in you? And how much time and effort have you put into moving toward healing, forgiveness, and resolution?

Because we are wired for relationships, when our relationships sour, our sense of well-being can sour as well; filled with hurt and maybe with rejection and loneliness, we pull inward to protect our heart. We lose our ability to trust others. We start to distance ourself. We begin to fill our emptiness with other things like work, entertainment, addictions—temporary satisfactions that soon become emptiness again.

In relationships, we interpret what happens and how others respond to us through our early childhood experiences and the conclusions we made based on those experiences. When we encounter difficulties in our current relationships, we may get angry and blame the other person's failure to love us as we need to be loved. And it's true that they likely played a role in our relationship dysfunction. But more importantly, our relationship difficulties are also shaped by what's going on *inside* of us and the way in which we respond to others because of our filters.

The good news is that while we can't make others love us more or better, we can control our internal responses and make healthy changes that will grow our relationships.

Family Ties That Bind

No other relationship shapes who we are or how we respond to life and others more than our family of origin. It's in our family that our patterns of emotional reactions develop—our family sets the blueprint for all our other relationships. This doesn't mean we're doomed (especially if we come from a dysfunctional family), as we can change these patterns, but only through awareness and intentional work.

Simply cutting these family ties, creating physical distance, or avoiding our family won't work to change patterns. The attachment runs too deep. If we're struggling in relationships today, the core reasons are rooted in yesterday. And if we don't take the time to understand this important principle, we will continue to struggle with emotional pain, trust issues, or relationship problems.

In fact, *family systems theory* explains that the family is an emotional unit, and any changes to one member of the unit affect the others.[1] These changes will predictably cause a reaction and an adjustment by the other members to find some sort of homeostasis within the family unit. For example, one family member may be identified as the "needy" one, and so another member will step in to compensate and take on that "weaker" one's responsibilities.

To complicate matters, our human nature will constantly seek to find the balance between *individuation* (independence, autonomy, and personal agency) and *connection*. And in some families and in certain circumstances, these two forces can be opposing—pursuing personal differentiation versus the drive toward togetherness. Think about being a teenager, and the angst we each went through trying to find our own way and figure out our identity, our values, and our priorities.

Recall the times you argued with your parents or were shut down or criticized when you disagreed with them. The anger and tension you felt inside was this natural warring between wanting to have your own separate sense of identity and, at the same time, longing for the approval and acceptance of your family, to feel like you belonged.

We have to manage this natural tension and anxiety within our family of origin. We then enter new systems at work and with new families, friendship groups, and communities. Any unresolved issues we have within our family of origin will reappear in our new systems, and we will continuously try to work out our relationship anxieties and the push-pull tension we carry of our need for differentiation versus togetherness.

Remember, cutting ourself off from our family of origin (either physically or emotionally) isn't differentiation but actually reactivity to anxiety; it's our attempt to escape the family ties that bind, and we're only hiding from all the messiness of our family dysfunction. Until we've done our own work as individuals, we can't help but bring that anxiety and dysfunction into any new systems we join.

If we haven't taken time to work through our family of origin issues, then we will be at a lower level of functioning, and the patterns will repeat. Once we've learned to pay attention to our own anxieties and how they impact others and the anxieties around us, we can be a better leader, friend, partner, or parent.

Can you see that doing your personal work to deal with your trust and relationship issues can literally change the systems around you, whether in your family, community, or organization?

Our unhealthy patterns *can* change, but only through developing awareness and intentionally working to alter our approach to relationships. Again, simply avoiding our family won't change our patterns. We have to accept the reality of our family's dysfunction, which may include grieving the loss of our dream of what a loving, healthy family should be like. It may mean working through our pain with a therapist, especially if there's been abuse or trauma. And very importantly, it may mean letting go of our unmet expectations and our longing for our family of origin to love us the way we want and need. It definitely means recognizing that any current problems we have connecting with others in a healthy way are due to trust issues rooted in our past dysfunction.

Unresolved Trauma

Some of you reading this chapter may be starting to see how your early childhood experiences have affected you. Maybe there is underlying trauma triggering your reactions, fears, and responses in present relationships and situations. For many people who have experienced early childhood trauma, those memories can get repressed but then resurface years later when something triggers those traumatic feelings from the past. In my experience, unexplained depression, emotional distress, and panic attacks are sometimes ways our body demonstrates unresolved post-traumatic stress (or PTSD).

Some symptoms of PTSD include recurring and distressing flashbacks and/or dreams; intense psychological distress or strong physiological responses (e.g., panic attacks) when faced with internal or external cues that resemble the original trauma; inability to recall important aspects of the trauma; efforts to avoid any thoughts, feelings, activities, or situations that remind us of the trauma; hypervigilance and an exaggerated startle response; difficulty falling or staying asleep; problems regulating emotions; and unpredictable outbursts of anger, recklessness, or self-destructive behavior.[2]

While avoidance is a natural response to anything that's painful, it's also kryptonite to your mental health.

If these symptoms resonate with you, don't ignore your body's signal to get some help. While avoidance is a natural response to anything that's painful, it's also kryptonite to your mental health and will absolutely stall your growth and interfere with the health of your relationships with God and others. I would strongly encourage you to consider seeking a qualified psychotherapist who treats PTSD to help you work through what is going on with you right now.

Regardless of whether specific, repressed memories are contributing to your symptoms, if you've experienced childhood traumas, it may be helpful for you to process those early childhood experiences. You may find relief from your symptoms just by processing them, but you may also end up discovering repressed traumatic memories that also need to be resolved.

Unresolved trauma will often remain locked in our brain but can—like a decrepit barrel of hazardous waste—"leak toxins" that lead to physical and emotional symptoms. Even if we don't consciously recall the trauma, we may find ourself reacting strongly to situations that otherwise wouldn't be such a big deal. It's vitally important to resolve this trauma so that our brain, body, and emotions have a sense of resolution. We can't change the past, but we want to be able to digest the important lessons that are part of experiencing life's challenges—and let go of the fear, shame, or lies about ourself that have been locked up inside us. Often, people will experience a sense of freedom as the trauma no longer holds them back from experiences or relationships they long to pursue.

There are a number of trauma recovery techniques that are quite effective in helping us move toward this healthy resolution. But make sure that the therapist you choose also teaches you techniques to help you stay grounded and in control of your emotional responses so that you can *safely* process through your trauma with that therapist. You don't want to be retraumatized by your therapist! Your emotional safety ought to be of the utmost importance to your therapist and must be established and maintained to ensure you are dealing with your trauma in a therapeutic and safe way.

Keep in mind, also, that trauma therapy isn't meant to be a "witch hunt" of discovering the facts of what actually happened. Memories are very susceptible to distortion.[3] There's no way to go back into your past to verify the specific facts of what you experienced, and so trauma recovery is more about resolving your symptoms and helping you come to a place of acceptance and peace. Don't spend all your energy trying to remember the details of what happened to you. Often, the more you try to remember, the more frustrated and depressed you will get, especially as you start to overly focus on trying to find the "answers." Instead, focus on the symptoms that need resolving and allow your mind and body to naturally bring forward what needs attention.

For Christ-followers, it's also important to remember that nothing takes God by surprise because he knows everything, so trust in his timing as he brings forward traumatic memories that need to be resolved. And if your symptoms are generally resolved and you're beginning to experience genuine peace and joy in your life, accept the ambiguity of not knowing all the answers this side of heaven. Give over to God those who have harmed, abused, or traumatized you, trusting it is up to him to deal with them. It is not up to you to make sure they know what they did or that they pay for what they did to you. Focus on what *you* can do to break free from the traumatic experiences of your past and then choose to let go of the rest.

If you're still hesitant about the idea of seeing a stranger to work through such intimate and painful memories, know that deep wounds are *not* something a spouse can fully help with, or even a close friend. While your loved ones can play a very important role in your healing, attachment injuries create insecurities that can push loved ones away and demand too much from them, which only exacerbates insecurities about rejection.

In therapy, often for the first time, clients can begin changing gradually, little by little, through a healthy attachment to their therapist. They begin to heal and develop the emotional capacity (and rewire their neural pathways) to connect well to others. The tangible warmth and care of a listening ear with wisdom and encouragement can help us experience God's love. One of my personal mandates as a therapist is that I represent tangible love to others so they can deeply experience it and begin to internalize it. Whether you choose counseling or not, opening your heart to others and sharing your painful secrets and wounds with another safe person is vital. Choose healing, and in that, begin to uncover the essential *you* buried under the pain and trauma. You are so worth it.

DIGGING DEEPER

Please keep in mind that the questions below are not meant to replace psychotherapy, especially if you are realizing you have some unresolved trauma. Rather, these questions should function as a gentle way to begin thinking about how your past may be affecting your present and your future. If you find even these questions triggering and are flooded with overwhelming emotions, or alternatively are blocked and can't remember much of anything and experience numbness, stop right away, do some deep breathing, and get professional help.

1. List all the important relationships in your life, past and present. Think about the issues you had/have with these relationships and consider whether there are any patterns to your issues.
2. How easily do you trust others? Think about past relationships where trust was broken. How did you handle that?
3. When you have a breakdown in a relationship, how do you usually handle it? Do you avoid and begin to distance yourself from that person? Or do you become anxious and pursue them to resolve the issue as soon as possible?
4. Do you have any trustworthy people in your life, those with whom you can be vulnerable and share your intimate secrets? If not, why not?
5. How would you describe your relationships with your primary caregiver(s) as a child and currently, if they're still in your life? In what ways do those relationships affect your current relationships with your partner, children, friends, or coworkers (in positive or negative ways)?

6. How would you describe your family system and how the anxiety between individuation and togetherness was handled? What anxieties do you think you're carrying today into your current systems, such as your family, work, friend group, or community?

The Stories
We Tell Ourself

Elaine came into my office and slumped down into the chair, head low, unwilling to look me in the eye. I could tell right away that it had been a bad week for her. We sat in silence for a few moments before she finally looked up at me with tears in her eyes.

"I don't know what to do," she said softly. "He just won't stop yelling at me, no matter what I do. I tried to do what you said and walk away, but it made him so mad, he punched the wall. Then he took off and got so drunk that he didn't come home at night. I don't know where he went, but when he came home, he stunk of booze and perfume. I don't even want to know what he was doing."

My heart sank. Elaine had been my client for several months, and although she was occasionally able to admit that her husband was abusive, her conservative Christian upbringing was forcing her to stay in the marriage. She struggled to see that emotional and psychological abuse was just as damaging—if not more—than physical abuse. Because her husband never physically hit her, she could not acknowledge the devastating impact his abuse was having on her emotional, spiritual, and psychological health.

It didn't help that most of her family was against her leaving him and instead encouraged her to forgive him and to try harder. And the worst thing of all? She continued to blame herself and take responsibility for their fights with a lot of "if onlys." *If only I didn't argue back. If only I hadn't forgotten to clean up the sink right away. If only I hadn't been so tired that I didn't have sex with him.*

After the self-recrimination, Elaine would cycle into shame-based ruminations of how it had been her choice to marry him, even after her friends had cautioned her about the red flags they saw. She made her bed, so she had to lie in it, right?

Like many victims of abuse, Elaine believed it was her fault. The top three lies that a traumatized person often believes are: *It's my fault. I am not safe. I have no control.* Those lies were keeping Elaine trapped in an untenable, toxic situation. They also kept her in a place of powerlessness, which opened the door to ongoing abuse and victimization.

Elaine didn't realize her internal narrative—her belief system about herself, her husband, others, and God—was keeping her trapped. Consequently, no matter what I said to her, she experienced only temporary encouragement and relief, as her internal filters continued to distort her interpretation of reality. She felt like it was her fault and she had no control over her circumstances, so she acted in a way that confirmed her own beliefs.

Yes, Elaine needed healing from the trauma she had experienced, and part of her healing also required external changes in her circumstances and life choices. But before Elaine could take any action to change her circumstances, she needed to change her internal narrative.

Our Dang Biases

Remember what we talked about in chapter 1, about our instincts and how they create biases in our brain oriented to our survival? As a result, there really is no such thing as complete objectivity.

Everything we experience and do and put out into the world goes through the filter of *me*. And because we are feeling, interpreting, meaning-making creatures, we will always have cognitive biases in how we view the world, ourself, others, and God. These biases can significantly distort our thinking, influence our beliefs, and sway our decisions and judgments.[1]

Research on biases indicates that there are common filters to which we can all be susceptible.[2] At my last count when searching the web, more than 175 biases have been identified, but I'm sure many more are out there, because we certainly are inventive creatures. As I go through a list of the most common biases we see every day, take note of which ones are your favorites (and maybe as a party trick, you can even tell others *their* biases).

My personal go-to bias is the *confirmation bias*, which is the tendency to pay attention to information that confirms our existing beliefs and ignore data that would contradict those beliefs. My echo chamber is so cozy and comfortable and doesn't require me to do the hard work of being open-minded and curious. And hey, it makes me feel good to be right all the time.

Another common bias is the *actor-observer bias*—another one of my personal faves—which is the tendency to ascribe blame to others (*internal* attribute) when explaining their actions, especially when things go wrong, and to blame circumstances (*external* attribute) when it comes to our own so-very-innocent actions. Because we can observe our own thoughts and actions but can't observe others' thoughts and motivations, we tend to focus on the situational causes for our actions but guess at the internal characteristics that lead to others' actions.

Similarly, our *self-serving bias* merrily allows us to give ourself credit for successes but conveniently permits us to lay blame on others, circumstances, or just plain bad luck for failure. Unfortunately, these two biases can get us into a whole boatload of trouble in relationships, as they form some of the most common ways people misunderstand each other.

Another filter we often employ is the *halo-horn effect bias*. We can express a halo (positive) bias toward someone we meet if we feel a positive connection with them, often based on very superficial data like appearance, social skills, and confidence. This bias then colors our judgments about them, so that we're likely to focus on seeing the good in them, even in the face of bad behavior. For example, one common research finding is that we will view someone who is physically attractive as smarter, kinder, and funnier than a less attractive person.[3] Conversely, if we have an instinctive dislike of someone or they do something that rubs us the wrong way, we can interpret all of their actions through a horn (negative) bias. Unfortunately, because initial dislike is often based on very superficial information, horn biases can lead to discrimination based on a person's race, color, gender, sexuality, political affiliation, religion, and so on.

We also can experience the *anchoring bias*, which is the tendency to give more weight to the first piece of information we get about a person or a situation. This bias often impacts our decision-making and judgment, even after we get much more information later on.

We can also fall prey to the *false consensus effect*, overestimating how many others agree with our opinions, beliefs, values, and attitudes. This bias can make us feel good about ourself because we feel like we're right and others support our positions. And yet we are spinning a narrative about ourself and others based on wrong beliefs.

Once we've formed an impression of someone or drawn a conclusion about a situation, we often hate to shift our stance. That's because of the principle of *cognitive dissonance*, which is the mental discomfort we feel from holding two seemingly contradictory beliefs, values, or attitudes. This leads us into black-and-white, right-or-wrong, binary thinking that can keep us rigidly closed to different ideas, even when faced with new data. Cognitive dissonance blinds us to our biases because we aren't willing to face the truth of how often we flee uncomfortable feelings or experiences.

The reality is that life, humans, God, and the world are filled with nuance and subtleties, and there is so much we don't know and have yet to discover! A nonjudgmental stance of open-minded curiosity allows us to recognize our biases and be teachable, to cultivate the humility to admit our mistakes and ignorance, and to be flexible enough to shift our position.

Our Narratives

On top of these biases, we have a system of memories—both *implicit* (unconscious) and *explicit* (conscious)—that are fallible and influenced by what happens after the actual event, what we choose to pay attention to (our perspective of the event), what others tell us about the event, and even how we feel when we look at the event in retrospect. Contrary to what some people believe, our brain does not record events literally like a tape recorder but layers on its own interpretation and filters.

Memories are created through connections between our neural pathways, either by strengthening those pathways or laying new ones. Changes in the connections between the brain's nerve cells are associated with learning and retaining information. Our memories are also organized in a way that makes it easier to access them to make decisions, solve problems, or interact with others.

All that means there is both bad news and good news about our memories. Starting with the bad news: our narratives about ourself and our life are formed based on experiences we have from birth, even before our verbal abilities begin, and are filled with tiny pieces of data and experiences that link together. And because those childhood memories often remain unexamined (leading to childish misbeliefs that never get challenged by loving, mature adults who can give us wise perspective) and below the surface of our conscious awareness, we can have narratives rooted in pain, fear, and shame even into adulthood.

Remember what we talked about in chapter 1? We tend to focus more on negative emotions as part of our survival. So, guess what happens with our filters when we aren't intentional about examining them? They can lead to inaccurate and negative assumptions about ourself, others, or the situation we're facing, which can cause us to act in ways that are self-protective and unhelpful.

The good news is that because memories are created through connections in our neural pathways, and we can strengthen or form new ones, we can rewire our brain based on new information, new insight, and new wisdom. Those new pathways will impact our mental, emotional, physical, and spiritual health. The even better news is that we can choose which pathways we strengthen (and which ones we prune), and practicing that new insight or wisdom will strengthen the connections between our neural synapses.

This is powerful stuff! Our narratives are formed by our reconstructed view of our past, our perceived present, and our imagined future. Read those words again: *reconstructed*, *perceived*, and *imagined*. There is a ton of active engagement occurring in our brain—our thinking, our attitudes, and our perspectives form our narrative. Can you recognize the power in that?

Even back in ancient times, the apostle Paul recognized the power of changing our mindset when he urged Roman believers to "let God *transform* you into a *new person* by *changing the way you think*. Then you will learn to know God's will for you, which is good and pleasing and perfect" (Rom. 12:2 NLT, emphasis mine).

> Can you see how essential it is to deal with the lies, the denial, the wrong filters, and the narratives you've told yourself?

In other words, using more modern terminology by well-known sociologist Brené Brown, "The power of owning our stories, even the difficult ones, is that we get to write the ending."[4]

Can you see how essential it is to deal with the lies, the denial, the wrong filters, and the narratives you've told yourself? How important it is to consider the ways you internalize the messages you heard growing up and continue to live out? Think about the excuses you make. The victim roles you play. The powerlessness you live out. The way you feel stuck, cycling in and out of the same old, same old.

Changing Our Stories

Stories are an incredibly powerful way humans bring meaning to situations. They are how we inspire, teach, and remember important lessons and also how we communicate emotion, meaning, and inspiration to ourself and each other. Our human stories are also all connected to each other in a generational, cultural, familial, interpersonal way. Many of us may have simply accepted the stories we were told by our family, our culture, our faith community, or others. We then see our own story through *their* lens of pain, hardship, marginalization, racial injustice, or gender inequality.

That was certainly my story. Until I intentionally examined my personal experiences and the stories passed on to me by my parents, I unconsciously carried their narratives of hardship, voicelessness, shame, and marginalization. Even though I come from a long line of brilliant and strong women, we have all struggled with having doors shut and our voices ignored because of our gender, culture, and Christian beliefs (my family was converted to Christianity by a White missionary who inadvertently taught us from a white supremacy perspective). So even as I "succeeded" in many ways, I struggled with insecurity about my place at the table, and that insecurity played out in both the macro and micro ways I showed up and pursued (or didn't pursue) opportunities.

There is powerful research emerging about how people can break free, for example, from generations of poverty,[5] and the literal rewiring of their brains that is required for them to liberate themselves from the curses of the past. While we don't get to choose which family, community, culture, or faith system we're born into, how we respond and what we tell ourself determines the trajectory of our life.

Do you hear that?

It isn't hardship, per se, that forms our stories (as the tough stuff of life happens to all of us). Rather it's what we *tell ourself* when faced with hardship, marginalization, injustice, inequality, or pain. We *can* begin to take ownership of our own stories and reframe our beliefs.

Just as a writer can edit what they have written and decide to change a character's story, you can do the same for yours. It requires something called *cognitive reframing*, which is the ability to shift your mindset so you're looking at a situation or person from a slightly different perspective.

Think about looking through a camera's lens. We can choose to either zoom in or view what we see through a wider perspective. The picture's subject can be viewed and understood from different angles and distances. Reframing can literally change the way we think—and therefore the way we feel—about a situation or person.

The Power of the "Boop"

There's a very funny series on Apple TV called *Shrinking*, released in 2023, that follows a group of three psychotherapists sharing a practice. The way they operate is all sorts of wrong from an ethical and boundaries perspective, but I have to be honest, that's part of what makes the show so funny for me. The show's ironic humor is part of what makes some of its messages more palatable, as it deals with very serious topics such as grief, trauma, mental health, and broken relationships.

Without giving too much away, one of the main characters suggests to one of his clients, who is stuck in an abusive and dysfunctional marriage, to just *boop*. He uses this word because the client is feeling overwhelmed and powerless to change her circumstances. What he's encouraging her to do is just make a *tiny shift* in her usual response or action. This *boop* is whatever small thing she can handle doing each day, but over time, the *boops* can add up to a whole new direction in her life.

Think of it this way: if you can remember your math lessons about angles, picture making a small shift, increasing the degree just a little; you know that as the line goes forward from that new angle, the distance from the baseline will become greater and greater until, eventually, you've made a very significant shift in your direction.

Sometimes these small degrees of change can take a lot of time, because the pathways in our brain are so ingrained they're like ruts in the road. And they may also require ongoing accountability, because we often don't even notice our habitual unhealthy responses. This philosophy is part of the power of groups like Alcoholics Anonymous that require self-honesty, accountability, and support with people who understand the struggle to overcome addictive behavior—to undo and change response patterns.

So, keep in mind, changing our narratives will take time, repetition, and awareness. But this journey also comes with a sense of hope. Change *can* happen. We get to dream about a present and a future we'd love to see as part of our stories. And while I don't ascribe to some of the pop psychology out there about "manifesting" our future, there is plenty of research on the *power of the self-fulfilling prophecy* that demonstrates how our beliefs can impact our outcomes.[6] As its name sounds, a self-fulfilling prophecy refers to the fascinating phenomenon, demonstrated again and again in research, that our expectations for ourself or others can bring about that prophesied or expected behavior.[7] Yikes!

Mindful Intentionality

Have you ever tried to do a home renovation? Not me! But I was an observer and sage advice-giver while my husband, Peter, renovated our house. Thankfully, he's also a civil engineer and is analytical and organized. But before the renovations could start, we had to have a clear vision of what we wanted. Now *that* was my department. I spent hours online looking at different colors, styles, and designs and went to paint stores to get paint chips. We also visited flooring stores and other stores where there were model designs we could walk through, touch, and experience.

While I was dreaming and designing, my husband was measuring and making charts. He was also tracking all the possible expenses on a spreadsheet, getting quotes for different kinds of materials. And he was in continual communication with me, because there was the dream vision and then there was reality, based on our budget and on what materials were available and easier for him to use.

My part was done pretty quickly, because it was just the vision. Once we agreed on that vision, Peter's part kicked in big-time. He had to think through all the various steps of the renovation, and he also had to pivot when things didn't go according to plan.

> **We need to have a vision for who we want to change into, and specifically what behaviors, thoughts, and feelings need to change.**

One vivid memory I have was seeing the rotting subfloor underneath the floor he was building. That new floor ended up taking more time and money to deal with than we had planned. Boy, did I do a lot of reframing throughout that project! I began to see our renovation journey as one of adventure and discovery, because as we dug deeper and deeper into our old house, we could see its history in the layers.

Imagine if we hadn't had a plan or budget and just went willy-nilly into that project? The wisdom found in Proverbs reminds us it would be foolish to start a project without a plan: "Do your planning and prepare your fields before building your house" (Prov. 24:27 NLT).

And that was just a physical renovation. How much more do we need to plan before launching into a renovation of our heart, mind, and soul? Often just knowing we need to change is not enough. We need to have a vision for who we want to change into, and specifically what behaviors, thoughts, and feelings need to change.

So, when we are shifting our narratives, it really helps to have a vision of where we want to end up. This isn't about saying to yourself, *I want to be rich, famous, and run a Fortune 500 company* but rather thinking about the person you want to be. You are the central character of your story—the one who has power, agency, and resilience; the one who is growth-oriented and committed to doing the hard work; and the one who *gets* to be that hero or heroine you know you can be.

For some of us, thinking about who we want to be is hard. If we haven't been affirmed much in our life, we may not really know ourself well. That's totally okay. The process always starts from *where we are*, not where we wish we were. If this is you, perhaps think of the person you *don't* want to be instead. Think about what things in yourself and your life you'd love to change. Be as specific as you can.

But before you can redo, you need to undo—to un-become before you can re-become. This is an ongoing process, and it will take your lifetime to work through the layers of misbeliefs, biases, and negative narratives that continue to pop up. Just keep in mind that we don't know what we don't know. Take an open-minded and curious stance, step back and try to see yourself objectively, and, *without judgment*, begin to untangle your narrative.

Don't be afraid to give trusted people—who love you, believe in you, and really know you—the permission to call you on it when they hear you say or do something that clearly indicates some negative thinking patterns. And give yourself lots of grace. This will be a messy, nonlinear, many-layered journey!

Do what you can with the Digging Deeper section below, but I would encourage you to come back to these questions again and again as you continue to dig out the gunk that hides the beauty of your essential self. Make sure you give yourself time to self-reflect—and lots of grace. These questions are not tickity-box activities; they will require reflection, self-observation, tracking, and getting feedback, again and again and again.

• • • • • DIGGING DEEPER • • • • •

1. Take some time now to think about your story—not the "facts" of your life but what you tell yourself. What are some common phrases you use when you describe your

life or yourself? Think about your family life growing up: what were some messages you heard frequently from your parents about themselves and your family, including the generations before you? Does this narrative reflect your current reality or imagined future?

2. What might be some biases you fall prey to? Any favorite ones? (If you have a hard time with this one, feel free to ask a trusted person in your life—they see them for sure!) How do these biases impact your beliefs about yourself, others, the world, and God?

3. What faulty filters might you have about yourself, others, the world, and God? As a start, here are some common ones: *I am too much. I am not enough. I have no choice. It's always my fault. You can't trust anyone. The world isn't safe. You're on your own. In the end, it's all up to you. God has way too many rules—I'm always messing up. I can't let God down / disappoint him. God is angry with me.* There are many, many more. As a way to help you start tracking, keep a journal of when you have "bad" days and feel "yucky." What thoughts are going through your mind? What misbeliefs or lies might be underlying your bad feelings? What limiting beliefs do you have about yourself? (*I'm never going to change. I can't [insert here]. This is just the way I am.*) You will soon find that themes will emerge as you keep track.

4. When you think of the people and the environments surrounding you, do you feel they support your growth? Or do they keep you stuck in a negative mindset? What about the media you consume? The movies you watch, the books you read? Surrounding yourself with people who actively support your growth while setting strong boundaries against people or situations that try to keep you stuck in a negative mindset will help you develop healthier filters and responses.

5. Now think about the story you *want* to tell yourself. What is your vision for your imagined future? Be as concrete as possible. For example, *I want to improve my physical health by joining a gym and exercising. I want to go back and get my degree. I want to start counseling or coaching to help me grow.* The list of desired changes can be as long or as short as you want it to be. It's not about getting it all right but about coming up with a clear vision with clear goals. It helps to add in realistic timelines. (Remember, it takes around three months to break a habit, so keep that in mind![8]) And also, give yourself lots of permission to pivot and change your mind.

6. Remember the power of the *boop*. Pick one area to begin working on and start booping. Maintain an attitude of experimentation—nonjudgmental curiosity—as you try it. And remember to reflect and track. For example: *That worked. That didn't work so well. When I did that, it made me feel like this.*

Fake It Until You Make It

Max looked like an entirely new man. Literally. Beyond his new color-streaked razor haircut, bushy beard, edgy clothes, and tattoo sleeves on his arms, he even had a different swagger to his walk as he came into my office. I hadn't seen him in several months, and during that break he had switched jobs from being a high school teacher to finally pursuing his dream of becoming a chef.

Instead of the soft-spoken and gentle demeanor I was used to seeing, Max was now projecting a much more intense persona, punctuating his speech liberally with curse words and waving his arms animatedly while he talked. He sat on the edge of the couch as he spoke, and the energy of his body language was palpable.

I could not be happier for Max. He told me about all the glowing feedback he was getting and the favor he seemed to be gaining with his boss. But as he continued talking about his successes and opportunities to showcase some of his own recipes, I began to sense an edginess to him and cynicism I had not noticed before.

When he paused for breath, I said, "Max, this is such exciting news! I'm so happy and proud of you for taking this big step.

This is huge! But wow, everything you had to do to get to where you are today . . . I'm thinking that as much as you wanted this career change, it probably hasn't been easy for you through the transition. How have you been doing in the midst of all of this change?"

Max paused, and then he sat back in the couch and sighed. I could see some of the energy draining from his body, and his demeanor shifted as he thought about my question.

He then told me he hadn't been sleeping well for weeks, and his anxiety was escalating. But he didn't know why, especially since he was so happy with his new career. He was well-liked by his peers and fit right in, even though he had been initially fearful that they wouldn't accept him because he wasn't like them.

At first, he figured his sleeplessness and anxiety were just the result of the long hours and hard work, but then Max started to wonder if there was something more. Maybe the huge amount of effort he put into trying to fit in with his peers was weighing on him, or maybe it was the stress of trying to prove himself to his boss. Perhaps it was the pressure he felt with each success to keep "knocking it out of the park." As he mused out loud, Max shared with me the many sleepless nights he spent ruminating about his recipes, and the countless hours he spent researching, tasting, and refining his dishes. It was never-ending. He felt like he could never relax because he had to keep outdoing himself. And it was even more exhausting because he felt like he always had to be "on," to project this image of confidence and brashness while hiding his anxiety and fear of failing.

Buried beneath the confidence and competence Max projected was a growing anxiety and insecurity that he was just one step away from failure, and one failure away from being exposed as a fake. Oh, he could puff up his chest and pretend he had it all together, but deep down, if he was really honest with himself, he felt like it was all just an act.

Max's speech slowed down, and he seemed to become more tentative and unsure of himself as he spoke, even physically shrinking into the couch. But even though he appeared beaten down, I could sense that this was a holy moment. Not only was Max at a breaking point but he was also at a pivotal place in his growth. While I knew that right then he only knew he was physically exhausted, I could sense his soul speaking to him and letting him know he was tired. Tired of faking it. Tired of wearing all the masks. Tired of having to always perform. Max was finally coming out of the shadows.

What If You Don't Like the Real Me?

Right now, dear reader, you may be doing everything in your power to mask your insecurities, even from yourself. You've suppressed those uncomfortable, anxious feelings for so long that you're not even conscious of feeling insecure anymore. And so you deny the possibility that you're faking it.

But I see that denial for what it is: it's your survival instincts kicking in to protect you.

I see you.

Everyone, to a number, struggles with this.

And actually, it's *because* of our fears and insecurities—no matter how much we deny them—that we learn early on to hide our vulnerabilities and fears. Our fears cause us to pretend we're fine; we remain trapped in this cycle of suppressing our true feelings and then needing to perform. We're so afraid we will be rejected if others really know what is going on in our lives. And so, we hide.

Deep down, maybe you're feeling like it seems like nothing you do will ever be enough. The tapes that play in your head say that if people really knew what was going on inside you, they would lose respect for you. Maybe you keep trying to pretend so that you can try to make everybody happy, including God, and you are completely exhausted physically, emotionally, and spiritually.

You're playing those roles, juggling those masks you have to wear, hiding your pain—while the pressure to pretend that you have it all together only seems to increase. Are you—like me—tired of all of that?

When We Started to Pretend

Remember in chapter 7 when I talked about family systems theory and the tension between the need for both individuation and connection? Wrestling with this tension happens throughout our lifetime, but never more so than during our adolescence. You see, adolescence is when we begin to develop abstract reasoning and an awareness of what's going on around us. We start to see that adults sometimes have their own personal agendas as they relate to us. We also begin noticing that adults don't always practice what they preach. And we start to question their values because we see that those values don't always make them better or happier people.

Think about yourself as an adolescent. What was happening in the world *around* you? What was happening in the world *inside* you?

What changes did you have to navigate as you were growing up and trying to find your place in your family, community, and broader society? Maybe you watched the world become increasingly fast-paced and competitive, and access to information and news become lightning fast through the internet.

You likely navigated societal values that seemed based primarily on your

1. *Performance*: how well you did in school, at work, at sports, and at church.
2. *Conformity*: how well you conformed to the expectations of others.
3. *Image*: how you looked to others, and what they thought of you.

On top of all that, as the world outside was changing during your formative years, you were also going through a world of change *inside* your heart.

As an adolescent—during the season you were attempting to individuate from your family of origin—you wrestled through three major tasks. Living your fullest life, being the best version of yourself, and living as your essential self depended on your successful navigation of these three tasks.

First, you tried to find your sense of *identity* (*Who am I?*). Adolescence is a time of discovering who you really are as God created you to be, who you are on the *inside*: a unique, special, one-of-a-kind treasured child of God. But unfortunately, if you inadvertently bought into the performance-based, image-based values of who you were on the *outside*, your essential self would have gone into hiding. Being different wasn't all it was cracked up to be.

Second, you developed your sense of *autonomy* (*What am I capable of?*). During adolescence, you developed your sense of personal power, the ability to choose for yourself and to take responsibility for your choices and your own life. This is a huge part of healthy development, yet many people get stuck here, either through learning to take power in an unhealthy and even harmful way, or through passively allowing others to choose for them. I see so many lost people who haven't successfully achieved this stage of development. (Sigh . . . who am I kidding? I see that in myself sometimes.)

And third, very importantly, you would have been searching for that sense of *belonging* (*Where do I fit in?*). This was a time of developing and nurturing your relationships, building your community, and developing deep intimacy with others in your life. Unfortunately, during adolescence you likely joined clusters of a number of social groups, rather than having consistent and deep friendships with any one group.[1] These relationships were likely more superficial and were for the purposes of survival rather than nurturing. In fact, you may have experienced some of your most painful relational experiences during your adolescence as you tried to rely on your so-called friends for that sense of belonging but ended up feeling abandoned and alone as relationships fluctuated. Remember, those friends were also trying to survive, and survival meant taking care of the self, even if it was at the expense of others.

If you haven't yet worked through your relational history of hurts and unmet needs, this may be where you're still at with your friendships and connections. And this may be a place of much-needed healing and growth for you.

● ● ●

As teens trying to individuate from our parents, it also would have been natural for us to question and even temporarily abandon many of our parents' values, including their Christian values. This can frighten parents so much that they, in turn, become more controlling and protective, and so goes the cycle until things sometimes escalate out of control.

Parents will sometimes interpret this stage of individuation as a time of "rebellion" and will do whatever they can to rope their teens back into line. Maybe that was *your* experience. Many of your fights with your parents might have been because what you wanted came into conflict with what they wanted. That battle between individuation and belonging might have been very costly for you.

Many adolescents—to survive—learn how to live in layers and operate out of different identities. We may not have formed these identities based on who we were on the inside but on what would have helped us survive whatever environment we were in. We didn't know who we were, and since everyone seemed to be evaluating each other based on external behaviors, we took that as our cue to make decisions on how we would be. And that's why, as teens, we might have acted one way at school, another way at church, another way with our family, and still another way with our friends.

Sound familiar? Maybe this is still you?

Aside from your family of origin, did you grow up in a religious system that focused on not messing up and behaving "correctly"—following the tenets of the faith community? I did, and I was taught a version of our human sin struggle that emphasized we were all just one mess-up away from disaster (but for the grace of God), and therefore following Jesus was all about following the rules. I learned early on how scary it was to step outside of the lines, because that could mean rejection and loss of belonging.

But see, this isn't belonging—this is simply *fitting in*. Belonging is when you are accepted *as you are*, not for your compliance with the group rules. Belonging is an innate human need; we need to be part of something larger than us. Unfortunately, we often seek to belong by trying to fit in and gain approval, which can lead to a myriad of performance-based masks. And even worse, the pursuit of fitting in can be a barrier to true belonging, because we never show up as our God-given essential self. Instead, we hide. We live in the shadows.

As the psalmist lamented,

> We live our lives like those living in shadows. All our activities and energies are spent for things that pass away. We gather, we hoard, we cling to our things, only to leave them all behind for who knows who. And now, God, I'm left with one conclusion: my only hope is to hope in you alone! (Ps. 39:6–7 TPT)

The God Piece

Each of us may be at a different place in our faith journey, and we may view God in very diverse ways. We may even be questioning what we believe, experiencing doubt, or just trying to make sense of our life in the context of what we've been taught about God.

So please, be tender toward yourself.

I think that wrestling with our faith is a *necessary* part of our rebecoming.

Wherever you are in your faith journey, I'd like to invite you to think about the sheer beauty and diversity of everything in the universe, including us humans who—even though we share 99.9 percent of the same DNA—are completely unique, with no two of us alike. You *do* have a God-given essential self. Your *you-iest* YOU. Your imperfect, messy, broken, beautiful you. So very worthy of belonging.

But true belonging only happens when we present our authentic, imperfect self to the world, and we experience acceptance. And that acceptance comes first from our Designer, who was absolutely delighted and completely satisfied when he finished our design. And then, from that centeredness, our own self-acceptance is key to true belonging.

One of the most affirming passages that reminds me that I am *known* by God, to my innermost being, is Psalm 139:13–17:

> For you created my inmost being;
> you knit me together in my mother's womb.
> I praise you because I am fearfully and wonderfully made;
> your works are wonderful,
> I know that full well.
> My frame was not hidden from you
> when I was made in the secret place,
> when I was woven together in the depths of the earth.
> Your eyes saw my unformed body;
> all the days ordained for me were written in your book
> before one of them came to be.
> How precious to me are your thoughts, God!
> How vast is the sum of them!

This passage tells me that our identities were formed before we were even born, that God thoughtfully and creatively designed each one of us to be unique and loved, and that he was pleased with what he'd created. Our identity and value have *nothing* to do with our performance or image or even whether we conform to his rules. I might be labeled a heretic for saying this, but it's true: our value to God has *nothing* to do with our obedience to him.

He foreknew every one of our messed-up choices, and yet he still chose to love us. Your identity is not dependent on what you *do* but who you *are* as his beloved creation. As his child. Obedience is a fruit of our love for him, and our love for him is based on knowing that he loved us first.

I grew up being a "good girl" in a Christian home where I quickly learned to follow the rules. Whenever I did something wrong, I felt a lot of shame, and I hid my wrongdoing. I was never taught the concept of grace, so although I did understand that salvation through Christ was a gift, I believed that living out the Christian life as a good Christian was my job. It led to what I call performance-oriented Christianity. My spiritual life was all based on how well I could follow the rules.

When I entered my teen years, I was tired of trying so hard to be good, and it just wasn't a lot of fun anymore, so I began to slide away from God. I did some bad things and started loading the double whammy of guilt and shame onto my performance orientation. And so, I am absolutely not here talking about a transformed life from a standpoint of never having screwed up. I think that I am an effective therapist exactly because I *have* screwed up and struggled.

But please listen to me—this is so key for you to hear. What makes me effective as a therapist in helping my clients isn't my knowledge or expertise. It isn't even what we *do* together or talk about in my office.

It's about the *relationship*.

I listen to and care about my clients. I look them in their eyes, and I *see them*. I see beneath their bristling behavior, beneath their actions that try to push me away. And I cry with them. I listen to their pain, and I care about their heart. I don't judge them or lecture them.

In this sacred place of safety, where they know they matter and someone is there for them in a way that reflects the heart of God toward them, they begin to heal. Because I see them, they can begin to see themselves for who they really are. And out of that security of knowing that they matter, they begin to make wiser and better choices for themselves.

I also give my clients the freedom to choose as God gives us the freedom to choose, and I walk with them as their choices cause them pain or joy, and so they begin to learn the power of personal choice and begin to develop the autonomy to choose for themselves. People rarely intentionally choose badly for themselves but rather do so out of ignorance, fear, pain, or anger. Because I believe in my clients, they begin to believe in themselves, and they begin to long to do better with their lives.

Your choices today don't depend on how smart you are, how successful you are, or how popular you are. They don't depend on your ability to follow the rules. That's all external. Your choices depend on what's going on in your heart.

So, what's going on in your heart?

Have you been turning away from God and other healthy relationships because of anger, hurt, or disillusionment? Have you been choosing relationships that are unhealthy and hurtful to you because you thought that's what you needed to feel connected?

Your choices depend on what's going on in your heart.

Or has your Christianity become performance-oriented and just a matter of routine and rote obedience, because that's what you were taught would gain you acceptance and identity? You do all the right things on the outside, but there's no passion in your heart for God.

To be honest, I don't want anything to do with a God who only has harsh expectations and comes down hard on me every time I screw up. I don't want anything to do with a religion that's just about rules and how spiritual I can be with reading my Bible and praying.

Well, guess what? God doesn't want that either. God is calling out to each one of us to get to know him personally and deeply. Not as a command or a "should" but because he knows that our sense of belonging, our worthiness, and our capacity to see and become our God-given essential self can only come through connection with him.

Listen, I'm not telling you to sort out all your theology or your beliefs. I'm not even telling you to let go of skepticism about God. And I'm certainly not declaring you must follow a religious tradition to experience the truth of what I'm saying. I'm just asking you to *choose to believe* that God loves you, he chose you before the beginning of time to come into this world, he carefully designed every detail of your being, and then he let you loose into this world to live out your purposes.

Think of the most beautiful place you've ever visited. Picture it in your mind's eye right now—all the color, the breathtaking spectacle, the feeling of wonder you had inside as you took in the view. Well, all the beauty of this world pales in comparison to the treasure that is humankind, because of all God's creations, we are his most beloved, his pièce de résistance—we are his most precious creation. *We* are his treasured image bearers, and he calls each one of us by name. He knit us together in our mother's womb, tenderly and lovingly, and when he was finished, he was well pleased.

Please *choose* today to grab hold of that truth and let it be your guiding light.

The You Piece

The truth that you're loved by God will not infuse into the core of your soul if you don't live it out in your life or practice the habit of *self-acceptance*. You *will* continue to be susceptible to the opinions of others and base your worth on your external performance and "successes" if you don't tackle this very important step of growth.

Before I talk further about self-acceptance, let me first say that it is *not* the same thing as self-esteem. The American Psychological Association (APA) defines *self-esteem* as

> the degree to which the qualities and characteristics contained in one's self-concept are perceived to be positive. It reflects a person's physical self-image, view of his or her accomplishments and capabilities, and values and perceived success in living up to them, as well as the ways in which others view and respond to that person.[2]

Can you see how the self-esteem movement may have inadvertently caused us to have a false sense of our worth, one based on ignoring our faults, overemphasizing our strengths, and expecting great things to come to us by sheer virtue of our greatness? (Can you hear the narcissism in this?)

In contrast, self-acceptance is not narcissism or self-aggrandization, nor is it blanket acceptance of ourself without any desire for growth or change. The APA defines *self-acceptance* as

> a relatively objective sense or recognition of one's abilities and achievements, together with acknowledgment and acceptance of one's limitations. Self-acceptance is often viewed as a major component of mental health.[3]

It's a nonjudgmental stance of acceptance of both the good and the bad in each of us. Acknowledgment is key to acceptance, as denying our weaknesses or reframing them as something positive is not self-acceptance. Acceptance is recognizing the existence of our weaknesses without suppressing them. We certainly cannot address something we don't think exists.

True and healthy self-acceptance means knowing ourself well and accepting that we are human and a work in progress. It's accepting our brokenness and the truth that we will make mistakes, fail, mess up, hurt others, and misjudge. It's acknowledging we can be selfish, self-protective, self-promoting, and prideful and can choose our own agenda over what's best for others. But self-acceptance is also believing in our ability to grow, to learn from our mistakes, to take ownership for when we hurt others—to *do better.* It's an affectionate view of our strengths, our unique quirkiness, and our potential, and it gives us a genuine desire to use our strengths for a good purpose.

Research has demonstrated that while self-acceptance is the one habit most likely to lead us to overall happiness and life satisfaction, it's also the one *least* practiced by most of us! Researcher Dr. Mark Williamson, director of Action for Happiness, explains:

> Our society puts huge pressure on us to be successful and to constantly compare ourselves with others. This causes a great deal of unhappiness and anxiety. These findings remind us that if we can learn to be more accepting of ourselves as we really are, we're likely to be much happier. The results also confirm [to] us that our

day-to-day habits have a much bigger impact on our happiness than we might imagine.[4]

Research confirms again and again how important practicing self-acceptance is to our mental health, our capacity to deal with stress, our ability to avoid self-destructive behavior, and, most importantly, our ability to pursue self-improvement.[5] It is vital to our growth, to rebecoming our essential self. But like any skill, it will take daily practice to build the habit of self-acceptance.

DIGGING DEEPER

1. Take stock of your negative self-talk. You began practicing this in the last chapter, but this time, pretend you're a kind friend: What would you say to yourself to challenge your inner critic? Be as specific as possible and find evidence to prove your inner critic wrong. Remember, there can be some truth to your inner criticism that may require an honest examination of your weaknesses and faults, but your weaknesses don't diminish your strengths, and you don't have to act out of your weaknesses.

2. Spend some time highlighting what you love about yourself. If this is difficult for you, ask your RB group (or trusted friends) to list all the strengths they see about you in writing. Reread this list until you begin to believe it.

3. Ask yourself questions that are focused on a hopeful movement toward change: *What do I notice about myself that I would like to change? How would I like this change to look? Why do I want to change this? What is this (behavior, belief, or action) stopping me from doing/achieving? Who can I ask for help to change in this area?*

4. Identify what you want and prefer. Knowing your own values, preferences, and wants helps you respect yourself and

validate that your values and preferences are important and worth having.

5. If your faith journey is an important part of your life, let God be one of those faithful friends who knows you, loves you, and can help you see the positives in yourself. Get into a regular habit of quiet time with God, and don't be afraid to ask him to help you grow in your self-acceptance; keep a record of what he is showing/telling you.

High-Functioning or Over-Functioning?

The pungency of the smell emanating from the toilet was enough to make me gag. But it had to be done. So in I went, holding my breath as I rammed the plunger into the ancient toilet to try to loosen the blockage. *Hold breath . . . thrust the plunger around frantically . . . stick head outside the door to take in a gasping breath before going back in . . . repeat.*

Thankfully, this time around my amateur plumbing attempt worked, and I was able to get the toilet flowing again. I sprayed a few bursts of air freshener as a final touch. Then I went down the creaky stairs into the partially lit basement. (Oh no! Another bulb had blown; I made a mental note to replace it.) I looked at the leaking hose coming from the water tank and wrapped some more duct tape around the hose to try to stop the dripping. I then inspected the black mold growing on the wall and reminded myself to call the mold inspector to make sure it wasn't toxic.

I noticed the time and rushed back upstairs to get the front desk organized before the staff arrived. My office administrator,

Lynn, had taken the day off for a doctor's appointment, so I needed to make sure all the psychotherapists knew where their invoices were for that day. Lynn had shown me the paperwork the night before, and I knew that if I didn't make sure the therapists got it right, the front desk would be a mess when she came back in the next morning.

It was now 8:58 a.m., and clients would soon begin flooding into the office. I ran quickly to the waiting room, where I turned on the soothing background music to calm clients while they waited for their therapist. I pulled out the snacks and coffee and tea choices and arranged them on the counter, then rushed to the library to turn on the electric fireplace. Ambiance is so important to our clients' experience. While in the library, I noticed there were some books left on the table, so I reshelved them. One of the loungers was slightly crooked, so I straightened it to align perfectly with the other lounger. There, now that felt better.

I heard the door opening and closing with a burst of voices and laughter and knew that the therapists had started arriving. I quickly escaped to my office and closed the door. As I glanced down at the pile of files that needed to be signed off, I sighed. Another day at the office had begun.

As the executive director and supervising psychologist, I had a team of twelve psychotherapists, an office administrator, a bookkeeper, and hundreds of clients who came to our center. On top of that, this particular office was in a beautiful location we had dreamed about for years that ticked off all the boxes, in a serene setting with ample space to fulfill our vision. I was living the dream.

What could be bad about that? Ha! Because of my desperate desire to please my team and make their dreams come true, I had ignored the red flags of going forward with that location. And there were many.

Once we were in and past the initial excitement of seeing our vision come to life, I had to fight a growing sense of shame that I'd gotten us into this hot mess. Not only did I feel a sense of responsibility to my team but I also carried that burden for my husband and our family, because I had staked a lot on the success of this dream office.

Oh, we had some very funny stories of mishaps from our time at that location, and I have fond memories of how we all pulled together and built such a beautiful team while we were there. But unfortunately, we also had some scary moments and very big problems to resolve. I'm pretty sure that everyone other than me (because I needed to stay in a place of denial to cope) soon saw the folly of my decision, but because they could sense I didn't want to hear it, they went along with my delusions.

I felt all the weight of the world on my shoulders to resolve the problems and minimize the negative impact on my team and my family, especially since I was the one who'd pushed for the location. I felt like I had *no choice* but to shoulder the burden of responsibility as the leader.

And so, beyond the daily clinical care I provided to our clients, I was also supervisor, plumber, lightbulb changer, repair person, administrative assistant, file clerk, housekeeper, and cheerleader. Oh, and I was also raising a young family at that time, and I was determined to be the best mother ever. That meant I attended all the school events, made meals from scratch, soothed boo-boos, woke up in the middle of the night to clean up vomit, checked homework, ran around to five different stores to find *the* toy for Christmas, and made sure I pre-taught my children everything I knew from the field of psychology to ensure they would become the healthiest, most resilient people on the face of the planet.

And I was exhausted.

Any of this sound familiar? The details of your story may be different from mine, but are you also trying to "do everything" and carry all the burdens on your own?

When did our high-functioning ways become over-functioning?

When High-Functioning Becomes Over-Functioning

Many of us pride ourself on being high-functioning—able to multi-task, perform to high expectations, and do difficult things, again and again. In fact, I would say that our modern, industrialized, social media–obsessed world celebrates high performance at any cost. We love seeing and celebrating the glory of success, while ignoring or minimizing the cost to that person or their family to achieve that success.

From the first time we win a medal or badge as a wee toddler, we learn that the pursuit of success is *the* way to happiness and acceptance. Do one thing well? Oh yeah, how about two things? How about many things? How about everything?

We get affirmed for our high performance throughout our lifetime, and we move up the ladder into positions of leadership because of our ability to get things done, especially if we can do it all without complaining. We brag around the water cooler about how tired we are and how little sleep we get, as if somehow all that exhaustion means we get an additional badge of honor.

> **Burnout is largely an emotional world phenomenon, created by feeling responsible for things that are not ours to carry.**

And Christians aren't immune, as we pursue doing more to serve God. Bigger and better, right? We've managed to spiritualize burnout.

We can then ultimately feel trapped by all that we have on our plate, all our responsibilities around career and family. And we can suffer from feelings of guilt if we can't do it all well. On top of that, we get judged if we "fall short"!

Where did we go so wrong in our values?

High-functioning leaders or parents are driven by high expectations and can end up in this dance of over-functioning to compensate for gaps they see around them. And so, committed, conscientious people often burn themselves out.

What is over-functioning? It's taking responsibility not just for your own life but for the lives of those around you. The over-functioner is someone who looks like they have it all together. They are high-capacity, reliable, and typically viewed as a strong performer.

Characteristics include doing work you know you should delegate to others, feeling responsible for someone else's feelings and happiness, being overly focused on another person's problem, frequently offering advice to help others, worrying about others, having goals for others they don't have, and doing things that are someone else's responsibility.

Notice that over-functioning is not just about doing for others; it includes thinking or feeling for others in a way that interferes with their self-efficacy. This means that excessive worrying is a form of over-functioning, as is spending too much time thinking about how to solve another's problem.

Burnout is not simply a matter of working too long or putting in too many hours; rather, it is largely an emotional world phenomenon, created by feeling responsible for things that are not ours to carry. The solution, therefore, is not necessarily to do less (although that is often part of it) but to feel less responsible for other people's responsibilities.

The High Cost of Over-Functioning

We can know two things for certain about over-functioning. First, over-functioning is *always* driven by anxiety. Like a drumbeat in our subconscious, driving us relentlessly to achieve, this anxiety keeps us in hypervigilant overdrive. Fear of failure or letting people down nips at our heels, keeping us in high gear.

We even glamorize this type of anxiety and call it "high-functioning" anxiety! Is there even such a thing? Could it be that the anxiety fuels the perfectionism that leads to apparent "high" functioning? Or maybe the demand to be high-functioning drives the anxiety? Or both? Regardless, pairing "high-functioning" with "anxiety" almost certainly guarantees a trap that's very difficult to escape, especially if our sense of worth is tied to our need to be seen as high-functioning.

Second, over-functioning always leads to *someone else underfunctioning*. This should serve as a warning to parents or leaders, or those stuck in a codependent relationship with a partner or friend who regularly disappoints. Over-functioning guarantees we will remain stuck in dysfunctional patterns, as we are interfering with the under-functioner's growth.

How will they ever learn the skills or develop the resilience to handle their responsibilities if we're always stepping in and doing it for them? How will they grow if we're always making decisions for them or giving them advice so they don't have to think for themselves? How will they develop wisdom if we're always stepping in to solve their problems? How will they mature if they don't get to experience failure, disappointment, bad grades, or negative job reviews?

As a parent and leader, I get what it feels like to worry about the people you care for because you want them to succeed. I understand what it's like to want to protect our loved ones from pain, so we tell ourself, *It's just this one little thing I'm doing for them.* Just that extra editing to fix an email my colleague was going to send. Just that extra bit of advice to help my spouse get dinner going on time. Just that one call to make a doctor's appointment for my adult kid. It's just a little thing, right?

But while it might seem like over-functioning isn't that big of a deal, over time it can have a huge impact on not only ourself but our relationships with others and their own functioning. When we over-function, we're constantly on edge, in reactive mode, as we try to manage those around us and orchestrate the details of not only our day-to-day but the minutiae of everyone else's day-to-day as well. I'm tired even just writing that!

When we assume responsibility for "fixing" situations and rescuing other people, they don't have to do their part, which can be frustrating at best and damaging at worst. It's no wonder that, given their constant fast pace and self-sacrificing behavior, over-functioners are prone to burnout.

Overcoming Our Over-Functioning

The first step of overcoming our over-functioning is to build up our self-awareness of our own anxiety and how it motivates us to act. (Other ideas to help you track yourself are in the Digging Deeper section.) We have to recognize our tendencies to jump in to try to control or fix a situation for others, and ask ourself, *Where is this anxiety coming from? Why am I trying to control the situation?* By stepping back and asking ourself these questions before we act, we become more aware of how often we over-function.

We also have to be willing to tolerate the discomfort of letting things go. Ask yourself, *What am I worried will happen if I don't step in?* Allow those anxious feelings to come to the surface as you imagine the possible disasters that could happen, and begin to make friends with those feelings. And as you feel your anxiety, take time to breathe deep, pray, or go for a walk—whatever you do to help yourself calm down. You *can* learn to tolerate distress! (Keep reading, as I talk about self-mastery in chapter 13—an important chapter that will help you with the skills to manage your own anxiety and reactions.)

We have to recognize that over-functioning is a form of compulsive self-soothing, as stepping in *does* lower our anxiety—at least for the moment—until the next situation comes along. It really is about our anxiety, which means we can take responsibility for our own reactions and change our responses for the better. Otherwise, the actions we take or the words we say can reinforce this pattern:

I feel anxious for others.
I step in to say or do something to "help" them.
I feel less anxious.
I repeat.

By the time you recognize you're over-functioning—maybe by reading this—it's likely become a habitual, ingrained response resulting from your sensitivity to the needs of others and your anxiety on their behalf. Please have grace for yourself and recognize that it will take time to disrupt these patterns of over-functioning.

You will have to tolerate discomfort, and it will require tracking, practice, and accountability.

This is also a time to practice self-care. Stop white-knuckling it and pushing yourself to keep doing so much for everyone! Start noticing your exhaustion and how your body is coping with the stress of over-functioning. Ask yourself, *What do I need right now?* I do recognize the reality of life. You can't always just go to a spa, but you can give yourself permission to do acts of self-care.

Overcoming over-functioning will also require setting new *boundaries*, because you will be changing what you're willing to do for others. Evaluate all the things you do at work, at home, and at church. Analyze what's really yours to do and what are tasks you've taken on as part of your over-functioning.

Before you start making changes in your responsibilities and boundaries, you may have to have an honest conversation with your family or your team to let them know you've become aware of your tendency to over-function and your intention to change. This may result in some feelings of relief from your family and coworkers, but don't be surprised if you're greeted with anxiety. If they've been under-functioning, they may feel ill-equipped to step in to take on that responsibility. Also, you may have been over-functioning to manage their anxiety and fears. You may want to work with a coach or a family therapist if there is a fair degree of codependency, as you'll need help to untangle all of that. There may need to be a season of slowly letting go, as your family or coworkers learn the skills they need to take on the responsibility that's properly theirs.

If you're going *ding, ding, ding* as you've been reading this chapter, take heart! We can beat this together! I've also included a short questionnaire in the Digging Deeper section to help you self-assess whether you are an over-functioner. (For the full version of the questionnaire, visit my website, DrMerry.com.)

DIGGING DEEPER

1. Check off as many of the following items as resonate with you. Be honest. The more you check off, the more you are over-functioning.

   ☐ I worry too much about someone else.
   ☐ I offer advice before it's asked for.
   ☐ I feel responsible for someone else's emotional well-being.
   ☐ I do work I should delegate to someone else.
   ☐ I step in to correct someone else's work without telling them.
   ☐ I make sure my partner or my child wakes up/goes to bed at a certain time.
   ☐ I remind someone of any important deadlines or appointments.
   ☐ I am overaccommodating when people need to reschedule meetings.
   ☐ I steer my child/employee away from experiences that may result in failure.
   ☐ I mind-read the wishes of a family member without asking them if my conclusions are correct.

2. Observe how you behave and think when you over-function. What are you doing, thinking, and feeling? Does over-functioning increase or decrease your stress? Are the people around you resentful, or do they reinforce your behavior?

3. Think about where you are most likely to over-function. Is it work or home? Church? With your kids or partner? Are there places or relationships that cause you to feel resentful? What happens when you give that unasked-for advice or help? Is there a sense of appreciation?

4. Complete the full questionnaire available on my website, then print off your results and tape the page somewhere you'll see it every day (bathroom mirror, fridge). Set a goal to have one less over-functioning behavior each day. This practice will remind you when you're over-functioning, so you can try to stop the behavior.

5. Give a friend or family member permission to call you on your over-functioning! In fact, if you're feeling really brave, give someone a copy of your completed questionnaire to help them notice your over-functioning ways— and tell you about it.

SECTION 3

Transformation

*How Do We Live as
Our Essential Self?*

The Strength of Vulnerability

Jesse was known as "the crier." It became a bit of a running joke among his friends because it was so predictable. Did he see someone hurting? He'd start crying. Feel compassion for a person's grief? Crying. Long for change to happen in the city? Crying.

But this time was different.

His friends could sense Jesse was feeling heavyhearted, but they didn't know why. Like a lot of guys, they didn't know how to talk to him about what he was feeling, so they tried to joke with him to distract him. They brought him food and some beer, but he didn't seem hungry and only picked at his food. Though they were able to see a glimmer of a smile on his face occasionally when one of them was being particularly goofy, he remained mostly somber.

Even though they liked to tease him because they didn't understand him or his big emotions, they cared deeply for him and would do anything for him. He was their best friend and the leader of their group, so they figured they would just go with the flow and, hopefully, he'd be able to shake off his mood.

Jesse suggested they go for a walk, and the friends leaped at the idea, thinking that the fresh air would help.

As they walked, Jesse's friends tried to keep talking among themselves, pretending everything was normal. But the awkward silences became longer and longer as the night progressed. Jesse seemed deep in thought but would occasionally say something obscure, like something to do with wine or a vineyard. The guys didn't understand what he was getting at, but they figured it was something so profound and intelligent that it was beyond their ability to comprehend. The part they did get was that Jesse was telling them he loved them.

But as they listened to him, it started to sound like Jesse was talking like he was going to leave them. The friends looked at each other, frightened. This was getting serious. They whispered among themselves, "What is Jesse talking about? What does he mean by 'a little while'? I don't get what he's saying."

They poked each other to stop talking so they could try to listen more closely as they walked. It seemed like whatever Jesse was talking about was important for them to understand. He was speaking about grief and joy, but all this emotional talk just made their heads hurt. And yet Jesse seemed to be waiting for a response from them, so they said, "Okay, Jesse, we believe you."

Just then they arrived at a garden, and Jesse asked his three closest buddies to go in with him. They looked at each other, shrugged, and followed him in. But then Jesse dropped to the ground and began weeping. He seemed tortured, barely able to speak. Finally, he said to his friends, "My heart is completely overwhelmed and crushed with grief. It feels as though I'm dying."

Alarmed and frightened by his words, his friends looked at each other helplessly. They didn't know what to say or do, or how to help Jesse. They felt powerless in the face of his palpable pain.

Jesse went on to say, "Stay here and keep watch with me."

Feeling somewhat relieved that there was something they could do, they nodded. Sitting down, the three friends waited for their cue from Jesse. They watched as he went to a different part of the garden, and they could see that he was lying face down on the ground and praying.

This felt reassuringly familiar, as they knew Jesse liked to spend hours praying and usually came back refreshed and encouraged. That calmed their sense of alarm. They knew Jesse could be a while when he was praying, so they settled in for a long wait. After the ups and downs of what had happened over the last few hours, they were emotionally exhausted, and so, one by one, they began drifting off to sleep.

The rest of the night was a blur, and none of them could attest fully to what happened after that. They recalled moments of being awakened by Jesse and then falling back asleep—a couple of times, actually. Maybe that's why what happened next took them so completely by surprise. Or maybe it was part of the trauma response, in which memories are mostly fuzzy yet flashes of minute details are imprinted on the mind. Like the smell of the flowers on the olive tree, the jumbled sounds of shouting, the expression on Jesse's face, the feeling of terror. Regardless, they knew with great clarity their lives were turned completely upside down that night as, to their absolute horror and shock, Jesse was arrested by a bunch of police officers. Beyond scared for their lives, they took off.

The Cost of Vulnerability

By now, those of you familiar with the narrative of Jesus's last night before he was arrested and then crucified have probably guessed that the story above is about him. This retelling was done intentionally, because most of us who follow Jesus prefer to remember him as a powerful Savior who did miracles and stood strong for what he believed in. While this is true, we often forget or minimize how much of his power he displayed through his endless capacity to love big and feel big. And how often he chose to share his emotions, his needs, and his heart so openly.

We'd rather see him as a warrior than as a crier.

We'd rather skim over the parts of the Scriptures where Jesus was witnessed crying, or when he was so emotionally distressed he was physically unable to stand, or when he was letting his best friend lean back against his chest. It feels too uncomfortable to consider that our Lord could be so intimate, so vulnerable.

But true courage is the choice to live with our heart wide open. In fact, the original root of the word *courage* is *cor*, the Latin word for "heart." And in one of its original usages, it meant "to speak one's mind by telling all one's heart."[1]

Researcher and sociologist Brené Brown reminds us:

> Vulnerability is not weakness, and the uncertainty, risk, and emotion we face every day are not optional. Our only choice is a question of engagement. Our willingness to own and engage with our vulnerabilities determines the depth of our courage and the clarity of our purpose; the level to which we protect ourselves from being vulnerable is a measure of our fear and disconnection.[2]

When we witness vulnerability in others, however, we don't think *courage*. We think *weakness*. And it stirs up discomfort in us. We'd rather avoid that very uncomfortable feeling and back away.

We've lived a lifetime learning how to hide our emotions and keep our emotional distance from others so that we feel "safe."

As we discussed earlier, vulnerability means opening ourself up to a world of hurt. It feels far too costly. And so our shadow self steps capably in to protect us, projecting an image of confidence, competence, and strength. Our shadow self helps us to hide.

Yes, vulnerability costs us. It costs us in emotional pain, even sometimes what can feel like intolerable pain. It opens us up to relational hurt and rejection. We face the reality of devastating disappointment and lost dreams.

The Greater, Hidden Costs

But what we don't realize is the much, much greater cost of choosing hiddenness over vulnerability. When we choose to hide, we lose access to our essential self—the person we were created to be and the life we were meant to live. We live life sleepwalking. We reflect

God's glory less. And we experience his love, peace, and joy far, far less. As Brown says:

> When we spend our lives waiting until we're perfect or bulletproof before we walk into the arena, we ultimately sacrifice relationships and opportunities that may not be recoverable, we squander our precious time, and *we turn our backs on our gifts*, those unique contributions that only we can make.[3]

Avoiding vulnerability may seem like a good short-term strategy, but in the end it costs us tremendously. Brown goes on to say:

> When we lose the ability or willingness to be vulnerable, joy becomes something we approach with deep foreboding. . . . Once we make the connection between vulnerability and joy, the answer is pretty straightforward: We're trying to beat vulnerability to the punch. We don't want to be blindsided by hurt. We don't want to be caught off-guard, so we literally practice being devastated. . . . When we spend our lives (knowingly or unknowingly) pushing away vulnerability, we can't hold space for uncertainty, risk, and emotional exposure of joy.[4]

We can become so consumed by our need to avoid pain that we fear savoring anything that brings us joy. We're too busy waiting for the other shoe to drop. So rather than experiencing the heights of joy, letting ourself feel joy becomes a trigger of fear for us, because it makes us face all that we could possibly lose.

Brown also explains other costs of invulnerability, such as living without expectations of good things so that we can avoid feeling disappointed, low-grade disconnection from life and simply going through the motions of living, a pursuit of perfectionism and performance just to experience the shadow of satisfaction, and, worst of all, a numbing of our emotions. *That* costs us the most, individually and relationally.

> Numbing vulnerability is especially debilitating because it doesn't just deaden the pain of our difficult experiences; numbing vulnerability

also dulls our experiences of love, joy, belonging, creativity, and empathy. We can't selectively numb emotion. Numb the dark and you numb the light.[5]

Along with flatlining our experience of life, numbing also causes us a whole host of other problems, including chronic physical pain,[6] mental health struggles,[7] and a lower sense of well-being and quality of life functioning.[8] Numbing also affects our relationships, because emotional vulnerability is a necessary aspect of intimacy and connection. Once the initial euphoria of meeting and connecting with someone new fades away, we end up just going through the motions, which decreases our sense of joy and happiness in our relationships. I wonder how many of the broken relationships we see around us are due to a lack of emotional honesty, problems with intimate and emotional sharing, difficulties with open communication about our needs to each other, and emotional numbness.

Even worse, emotional numbness costs us in our *humanity* because it causes us to care less about the suffering of others,[9] and it increases the likelihood of psychopathological responses.[10] Could the problems we see in society that cause untold suffering, brokenness, and damage be linked to the closing of our hearts?

Could this perhaps be a big part of why Jesus chose to become human and walk this earth—to model the power of love and openhearted vulnerability and see millions of lives changed as a result? Vulnerability is true courage and strength. And this is how we're meant to live, as our essential self, made in his beautifully vulnerable image.

Counterfeit Vulnerability

In a world saturated with ready access to vulnerability research, I doubt there is anyone reading this book who hasn't heard about the power of vulnerability or authenticity. You may even have skimmed through the last few pages of this book, thinking, *Been there, done that. Check.*

So, I have to call this out. Well, to be honest, I'm calling myself out. Sometimes I'm pretty good at fooling myself into thinking I'm being vulnerable because I talk about my feelings openly and even show emotions in my facial expressions. But deep within my soul, where self-honesty lives, I know it's curated. I'm presenting my "vulnerability" in a way that's neat and tidy, wrapped up with a pretty bow, without all the jagged edges of my unresolved pain or my needy soul on full display.

My shadow self is very good at mimicking vulnerability, but *it comes from a place of performance* and the impact I'm trying to have on my audience. It also comes from a place of thinking I *should* be vulnerable, because isn't that what emotionally healthy people do?

Watch any reality TV show, follow any big influencers on social media, and I bet you'll see plenty of counterfeit vulnerability. Emotional vulnerability sells. It gets you followers. It gets you famous. The more you let it all hang out, the more people tune in.

Now, I'm not saying that what we see is all inauthentic. I'm just saying that it's a trend. And we need to do some serious soul-searching: Are we just following that trend, or are we truly doing the soul-digging we need to show up as our essential self, open-hearted and authentically vulnerable?

I want you to pause for a moment and ponder this more deeply. Don't skim quickly past this section. This is the pivotal point of true transformation.

Without vulnerability, there is no true transformation.

If I'm making you feel uncomfortable here, and you're starting to second-guess yourself, *good*. Linger here, in the discomfort. Feel the pull toward true vulnerability as you face the truth of how often you may have been faking it. Or maybe you've been able to avoid the fake, but you're a toe dipper—you dip one little toe into vulnerability and then pull back, way back. You tell yourself you're still "processing," but really, you're just putting it all back on the shelf to be avoided while you go back to your life of safety and numbness. It's making your head hurt, so you put it off once again.

Honestly identify whatever it is you tell yourself to avoid true vulnerability. Now, take a deep breath, because it's time to wade in. Pause and think through the questions below.

Do my friends know about my current struggles and worries?

Do I talk openly about my negative emotions, such as fear, disappointment, or jealousy, without trying to cover them up or deflect them?

Have I told anyone about the things I'm most ashamed of?

When I'm feeling sad or depressed, do I reach out to anyone for support or help?

Have I ever told anyone what I'm longing for when I feel needy?

Do I cry openly in front of others? (I'm talking snot-crying.)

Have I told others about some of my biggest failures?

Do I let myself feel hopeful and excited about new relationships or opportunities, even though things are still uncertain?

What am I most insecure about, and have I told anyone?

How painful was that? I must admit there are far too many questions in that list that make me squirm. I hope you also felt relief. Honesty is what we signed up for, right? Also, remember that you're not alone in your struggles with vulnerability, and going through this process connects us.

True Vulnerability

Think of yourself as a child (or if you have the privilege of a young child in your life, just watch them) and recall how open you were and how readily you let everything you felt show. How quickly you cried when you got hurt, how swiftly you ran to your caregiver for

140

comfort when you were scared or upset. How joyously you belly-laughed, and how often you expressed your delight and full-out exuberance when something tickled your fancy. How excited you were to wake up to explore the world, to engage your sense of curiosity and imagination. Or maybe you were a shyer, quieter soul, and were tenderly sensitive, crying easily in solidarity when you sensed the pain of others. Maybe you noticed other shy kids and were moved to befriend them, to make them feel seen. Maybe you were that child who enjoyed cooperating with others and making them happy.

Think about that sweet soul you were. Hidden behind your masks and performative behaviors, you're still there. Your birthright you, implanted by God.

Please come out of hiding.

Choosing vulnerability *is* the pathway forward.

In our shame, fear, and insecurity, we have been trapped by the lure of performance, people-pleasing, and perfectionism, and in that prison, we have allowed the fear of vulnerability to create a wall around our heart. But we can choose freedom and see what it's like on the other side of that vulnerability wall.

> **Choosing vulnerability *is* the pathway forward.**

True vulnerability is hard work, exposing our shame, our fears, and our insecurities. It requires humility and self-awareness. It means we have to ask for help when we're at our lowest or when we want to give up. It shows others our neediness and opens us up to rejection. Again and again.

Remember that story I told in chapter 1, when my friend hurt me deeply with her thoughtless words? My typical modus operandi would have been to suppress my feelings of hurt, pretend to her that everything was okay, and move on.

But instead, knowing that I needed to grow in my ability to be vulnerable, I did a brave thing and chose to talk to this friend in the midst of my pain. Rather than trying to process it myself and tie it all up with a tidy bow before I brought it up, I chose to be vulnerable and invite her into my messiness. Because, deep down, I knew I could trust her. And she was beautiful in her compassion for me, her sorrow at hurting me, and her genuine desire to know me. My hurting heart was knit together just a bit more than it had been before. And I was given the gift of an even more precious friendship with this dear lady.

You, too, can do this brave thing. I know you long to be seen, and *I* long for you to be seen. Your soul needs you to do this. The belonging you need can only come with true vulnerability, when you show up with courage and experience acceptance and grace.

> **As you allow yourself to be vulnerable with Jesus, you'll start feeling centered again, knowing that you're not an Other to him.**

When you feel othered, instead of retreating and shutting down or pretending that everything's okay, choose instead to bring your aching, hurting self to Jesus. And you and he—plus the little, hurting, hiding person inside you—can choose to sit together. Embrace his tender love for you and his compassion for little you, and you'll begin to feel peace. You can give the broken pieces of your heart to Jesus and invite yourself to cry in his arms. As you allow yourself to be vulnerable with Jesus, you'll start feeling centered again, knowing that you're not an Other to him. Practice vulnerability with him first, as many times as you need. I promise you he will never judge you or reject you. He *loves* you, and he *knows* you.

In the security of his love and acceptance for you, you can then choose to come out of hiding and be vulnerable with others.

Choosing Vulnerability Every Day

Now that we've reframed vulnerability as bravery—and, for Christ-followers, as modeled beautifully by Jesus—let's get to practicing it. Start small and take one brave baby step at a time. Think of it as a new habit you are learning, and practice, practice, practice!

To be more vulnerable, you must begin by knowing your inner world better. When I'm first working with a client on identifying their emotions, I will often suggest they look for an emotions wheel on the internet. It doesn't have to be an all-encompassing, professionally designed one. Just choose any one and get going. If that feels overwhelming, choose one that's designed for kids and has fewer choices. And then, at least once a day, look at that wheel and decide how you feel at the moment. And write it down. Keep track of it. Perhaps get colored markers to use for your different emotions, whatever it takes to make it interesting and engaging for you. This practice will help you better understand your internal workings—the emotions you feel.

Next, notice your triggers and reactions when something good or bad happens, and ask yourself, *What's going on behind my reactions?* Allow yourself to notice how you feel in different situations and where you feel it in your body. Then practice saying how you feel out loud (initially just to yourself). Don't worry if you feel awkward. This isn't about getting it "right"; it's about practicing emotional awareness.

Now, this is where it starts to get real: begin telling people about how you feel and what you need. Find a few trusted folks and let them know that you're trying to practice vulnerability (even telling them this is a step of vulnerability!) and are learning to identify how you feel and communicate it to others. Ask them for feedback on how your honesty is being experienced by them (another step of vulnerability!). Make sure to pick friends who love you and can be gentle with you. And give yourself lots of grace too, since this is a new skill you are learning, and it might be messy at times.

Remember, none of this can be done without risk. Try to maintain a growth mindset, with the acknowledgment that you will make mistakes. You're here to learn and use those mistakes as part of your growth. And in your risk-taking, you may experience hurt, judgment, misunderstanding, and rejection. In therapy, I teach clients to develop tolerance for difficult experiences as they build their resiliency to handle the ups and downs of life and relationships. In your courage to face the discomfort of your vulnerable feelings, you, too, are developing resilience and confidence that you can do hard things. You're also learning relationship skills, so important in your transformation (more on this in chapter 15).

The ultimate fruits of greater vulnerability include healthier relationships, better communication, more intimate connections with others, and a true sense of belonging. I promise you, it's well worth the effort!

• • • • • DIGGING DEEPER • • • • • •

1. Practice saying "I don't know" instead of being defensive, explaining yourself, pretending you understand, or arguing for your position.

2. Try something totally new and let yourself be bad at it. Pick something out of your comfort zone and, even better, do it with someone you know so you learn to tolerate "looking bad" in front of others.

3. When you're in an argument, be the first to apologize, and be as specific in that apology as possible. For example, rather than a generic, "I'm sorry I hurt your feelings," try, "I'm sorry I cut you off when you were trying to tell me about your day, and I hurt your feelings."

4. The next time someone says, "How are you?" instead of replying with the usual brush-off, trying telling them how you're *really* feeling.

5. Book some time with one trusted friend to share something personal with them that you've never shared before. Talk about something that is particularly tender and private.

6. Let someone know what you're learning about yourself through this book! Share some of your answers to the Digging Deeper sections.

Shame Resilience

Brandon sighed deeply as he slumped back into the couch. It had been almost two years since he'd first told me about his porn addiction. Over those two years, he would attend therapy faithfully for a few months but then disappear for several months at a time. Each time he came back, the shame monster would be sitting heavily on his shoulders, hissing at him for his weaknesses and his failure to overcome his addiction.

This time it was really bad. His wife had finally kicked him out, and he was camping out in his brother's basement. Unfortunately, this only exacerbated his feelings of depression and hopelessness, to the point that he was having suicidal thoughts. He was ready to give up. He knew he could never overcome his addiction. On top of that, in his wife's hurt and desperation, she'd decided she would no longer hold his secrets for him and had told their families, their priest, and people in their small group about Brandon's struggles with porn. Now he no longer felt safe with them.

I was the only person in his life with whom he was truly vulnerable about his struggles with addiction, yet during our sporadic sessions, I could sense he was sometimes holding back. There would be times I could see the truth in his eyes, even as he deployed a jovial demeanor to hide his pain and project that he was okay. It was like he would feel relief when he came in and confessed, but then real life would get in the way, and he would feel the weight of shame all over again.

I suggested many times that he join an addictions group, but each time he would brush off the idea, saying he was fine just coming to see me. But when he arrived at our session this time, he was ready to finally acknowledge that this was a lie; things had become much, much worse.

"Brandon, my heart is hurting so much for you," I said gently. "You must feel so very, very alone."

He nodded wordlessly, tears springing to his eyes even as he looked away from me.

"Listen to me, Brandon. You are still the same person you were before you became trapped by your addiction. Still the same wonderful, kind, and gifted young man. Nothing has changed about your worth and your value. Because your worth has never been based on your performance or what others think about you."

I took a deep breath, and then carefully confronted him. "But you cannot keep hiding your struggles from others. That is the *very thing* that is keeping you trapped. You cannot fight this alone. I'm so sorry that your wife took away your power to choose which trusted people to tell about your struggles, but the secret is out now. Maybe it's time to stop hiding.

"You did a brave thing when you first told me about your struggles, and you continue to be brave when you show up here to face the truth that you've slipped once again. So I *know* you can do brave. I'm just asking you to do another brave thing . . . one that is critical to your recovery." I paused and waited for him to look at me.

"Don't do this alone. You need to join an addictions recovery group, and you need to find a sponsor you can call any time you need support. Coming to therapy is not enough. You need to be with fellow recoverers who know what it's like to struggle. You need to hear their stories of triumph and also their failures. You need to know that you're not alone and that there are people *with* you and *for* you, no matter what. And you need these people in your day-to-day life, not just in a therapy office. You need a safe group of people with whom you can show up as your broken, struggling, hurting self, so that you can find healing. No more pretending."

By this point Brandon was nodding, tears streaming down his cheeks. Shame had lied to him and told him he had to isolate himself and avoid exposing his secrets at all costs. But he was finally realizing that shame was keeping him away from the very thing he needed, the thing we all need: to belong, *no matter what.*

Facing Shame Head-On

In the last chapter, we learned about true vulnerability and how to cultivate it. Vulnerability—with trusted people—is also an essential ingredient for shame resilience and finding belonging. Vulnerability is a nonnegotiable part of facing shame head-on and declawing its power over our life.

I shared earlier that I grew up as a "good Christian girl." But in my teens, hurt by a series of very painful experiences within my church, I'd had enough of religion. On top of that—what felt like the far bigger betrayal—was that God had failed to heal my brother, even after so much prayer. He had not come through. *I* did everything right, but God seemed to remain stone-cold, and *he* didn't do the right thing by me.

> Vulnerability is a nonnegotiable part of facing shame head-on and declawing its power over our life.

And so, even though I still "believed" in God, deep down I didn't trust him. I felt alone. My immigrant parents were already beyond overwhelmed trying to survive in a new country, and after losing their precious firstborn son who was supposed to be a pastor, they did not have the capacity to be emotionally available for me. I was literally left on my own to find my way.

I developed resourcefulness and independence that allowed me to forge ahead and make my own way in the world. But inside that outer shell of confidence and competence was a scared little girl who knew there was no one there for her. And in my teens, tired of religious restrictions that did absolutely nothing for me, I turned my back on God and went on my merry way.

I plunged into a season of rebellion, doing anything and everything I wanted: partying, flouting my parents' rules, experimenting sexually, and opening myself up to the dark world of pornography. I was still the good girl on the outside, playing the part every time I surfaced to my parents, but on the inside I was seething with anger, pain, and loneliness—and managing to lie to myself that I was just having a good time.

But it was ever so costly.

Shame had its tentacles firmly around me. I could not face the darkness within me, and so I strayed further and further from God. Fear became my taskmaster on top of that shame, and I felt like I had no choice but to rely on my own resources—my performance, people-pleasing, and perfectionism—to manage my life. Otherwise bad things would happen, and my life would fall apart.

Now fast-forward a decade or so. I'd built a successful career as a psychologist. I was married and expecting a child. I was mature enough to have left the rebellion of my teen years behind but was still far away from God.

But it was an interesting thing to have been raised in a faith tradition and now be expecting a child. I began to consider the life I wanted for my daughter. I don't think I had the spiritual maturity at that time to think about her personal relationship with Jesus and what that all meant. I just wanted to bundle her up in the safe cocoon of Christianity so that she would walk a straight path and receive God's blessings and protection. (I know; it's ironic, as feeling unprotected by God was the very reason I'd walked away from him.)

Regardless of the logic of my motivation at that time, I began walking my road back to God. Well, really, I sprinted down the road, plunging into full-out commitment to a local church and all the Christian activities I could get my hands on—Christian books, preaching on tape, serving in different ministries. (I was up to six ministries at one point; can you beat that?) I was going to be the most Christian person I could be.

Deep down, I thought I could wipe away all my dark years with penitential actions. But shame still had a firm grip on me, and it would not allow me to experience God's grace. Oh, I knew in my head he loved me, and I was forgiven. But in my scared, broken, damaged heart, I felt like I was a lost cause.

I would literally have nightmares about being exposed. I would wake up sobbing from horrifying dreams. By this point, I'd stepped into positions of leadership, and I began speaking at retreats and doing Christian counseling. The higher I climbed up the Christian ladder, the more terrified I was of being found out as a fraud.

But one night, while tossing and turning after being woken up by one of those nightmares, I began pleading with God to rescue me. I couldn't go on this way. And he answered me in a way that frightened me even more. I sensed him asking me to call my mentor and book some time with her. He wanted me to tell her every dark secret I was hiding. And I mean everything.

God knew I was desperate enough at this point, so I drove to my mentor's home in the early morning to speak to her in person. She sat me down and waited, sensing an important moment. My heart pounding, tears streaming down my face, I told her *everything*.

She listened patiently, and when I had finally poured out all my dirty secrets, she cupped her hands around my face tenderly, looked me in the eye, and said with such love, "Oh my dear, Jesus has forgiven you."

It wasn't anything earth-shattering she said but rather the palpable experience of her love and grace—her tenderness in the midst of my most shameful secrets—that finally broke the back of my shame. I still cry when I think about this pivotal moment in my life; I am crying now as I write this.

When grace comes into your life and God calls you to vulner-ability, it breaks through your walls, your defenses, your fears, and your loneliness. That is why I continue to follow Jesus; his grace has literally rescued me. Coming home to Jesus in all my vulnerable, broken messiness—and experiencing his love and acceptance—was when I finally understood what it was to belong.

The Practice of Shame Resilience

I wish I could tell you that, from that point on, shame no longer had a hold on me. But no; it wasn't quite so easy. Instead, shame simply slithered into other, deeper layers of my life, still just as hidden—maybe even more so. While I didn't feel the enormity of my shame anymore, it still had control over my life in much more subtle ways.

I will wager a bet that it has that same subtle control over your life too.

Breaking free from the stronghold of shame requires inten-tionality; we must face it down again and again and again. It requires the regular practice of shame resilience. Otherwise, it's like whack-a-mole: once we knock it out of one part of our life, it pops up in another.

You'd think followers of Jesus, the ultimate grace-giver, would have this in the bag—but no, not so fast. While studies show that having faith and some religious affiliation have a positive effect on our mental health and well-being,[1] people who struggle with chronic shame have trouble engaging in their faith practices and can struggle in their attachments to God.[2] So the solution to our shame problem is the very thing that can be a barrier to our freedom.

Shame resilience has been researched quite widely, and the re-sults reveal that it decreases depression,[3] improves our relation-ships,[4] improves our ability to bounce back from adversity,[5] in-creases resilience to overcome significant barriers to changing one's life circumstances,[6] and helps to overcome addictions.[7] Shame re-silience is key if we want to cultivate belonging—connection with our essential self and with others.

According to Brené Brown, the four habits needed to cultivate shame resilience are:

1. Recognizing shame and our triggers, how it sits in our body and how it makes us feel in real time.
2. Practicing critical awareness of all that's happening around and in us when shame pops up.
3. Reaching out to trusted others and telling our story so that we can actually come out the other side of the shame tunnel.
4. Speaking shame out loud and kicking it to the curb— bringing shame out into the light again and again. We get to normalize shame as part of life.[8]

It's clear from the research that shame resilience is a skill we have to practice, so that we can develop the ability to halt shame in its tracks. It will take our lifetime. I promise you, it does get easier to see shame as it's making its way through your emotions, thoughts, and actions, and you can get better at using strategies to stop it from hijacking you. And I will walk you through a process to help you practice shame resilience in a moment. But first, you must come out of hiding.

It's Time to Come Out of Hiding

Another pause moment here. There is a ton at stake. Lean in right now, and please hear me out.

Without shame resilience, our essential self cannot come out of hiding.

Let me try to explain. The most destructive form of shame we can experience is *internal shame*; that is, the shame that comes from within us, from our own *self-rejection*. This form of shame is caused by the discrepancy between our undesired "bad" self and our idealized "good" self. So much of why our shadow self remains fixed in our psyche is because of the terrifying sense of shame we feel at the thought of exposing our undesired self. And so, we believe we must reject that part of ourself.

Our undesired self came into existence at a very young age, after perceived rejection, hurt, and attachment wounds. These came to be when our caregivers would punish us for our "bad" behavior and we would experience their anger, withdrawal, or disapproval when we misbehaved or didn't meet their expectations. And our idealized self was born out of the praise and hugs and words of affirmation we received every time we were "good" and pleased our caregivers.

That's when our soul splintered. Good versus bad. Visible versus hidden.

And even more paralyzing? Our shadow self is secretly terrified that our essential self is really just our undesired self—unlovable, unworthy, and bad. Can you see why the battle is so fierce? Why we keep our essential self so hidden?

But can you also see that rejection is the very last thing our undesired self needs? There is a world of hurt, trauma, and pain that needs healing. And for healing to take place, we need to bring these wounds out into the light. Instead of seeing our undesired self as bad, can we see our self as hurting? We are broken and longing to belong.

May I remind you that your essential self is your very own God-breathed, beloved, precious self? Your essential self is not perfect, but you are still wise, humble, brilliant, quirky, and wonderful. Yes, your feet will still smell when you walk in your sweaty shoes. You will still have gas and constipation. You will still get angry, and you will still mess up big-time. Again and again.

But your essential self will pick yourself up and do better. You will continue to grow and mature. And you will never stop being loved. Your essential self will always belong. In all your human, stinky, messy glory.

Practice Makes Imperfect

Before I lay out a practice plan for shame resilience, can I ask you to do something?

There are many exercises you can access on the internet if you want more variety of skills to practice or you simply don't resonate with mine. Just don't use that as an excuse to stop!

Take out your phone right now and put a daily reminder on it. Choose a time when you're most awake—or most in need of a reminder—to practice shame resilience. Don't worry, this doesn't mean you have to stop everything and do all the steps every time your phone dings. It's just to help you keep the practice front-of-mind.

Next, make sure you've discussed with your RB group all the ways in which you're going to practice shame resilience together. (If you're doing this book on your own, text a few trusted friends right now and tell them you're going to practice shame resilience.) Put it out there so you have support from your people as you try these new skills; you're also alerting them that you'll need lots of grace from them as you practice.

Okay, here goes. We're going to do this as we would any new skill: by building each component part before putting it all together. And remember, this is not going to be a linear process but will have forward and backward movement, and lots of zigzags in between! Shame resilience is not all or nothing—either there or not—but is on a continuum between shame (fear, blame, and disconnection) and empathy (courage, compassion, and connection), and so this will be a lifetime of growth.

DIGGING DEEPER

1. For the first part of your shame resilience exercises, you're simply going to practice being aware of when you feel shame. Go back and read chapter 4 again, if it helps to remind you of how shame shows up. Hopefully, you've already worked through the Digging Deeper exercises from

that chapter, so you've already made a good start. Don't forget you might not actually feel the emotion of shame, so watch your behavior for anything that is shame-y. Every time you feel tension in your body, or you feel yucky, stop and ask yourself, *Is this shame?* Consider what's happening in your body when you make a mistake. Where are you feeling the tension? How do you feel when someone corrects you? Do you feel defensive or like you have to explain yourself?

At this point, don't worry about trying to stop your shame reaction. Right now, it's just about noticing when you feel shame. Keep track of it, and start to see if you can notice a pattern. Also see if you can figure out where shame shows up in your body. It might be an impulse to cringe or to look down or away from others. For me, I feel a hotness in my face and a sinking in the pit of my stomach. Oh, hello there, shame!

2. Once you feel like you have a pretty good idea of when you're feeling shame, you can move on to the next building block of shame resilience. This is when you start to observe and analyze. First, *What's going on outside of you?* What events, people, or conversations triggered that feeling of shame? Look for themes to those triggers. Next, *What's going on inside of you?* What harsh words are you saying to yourself? What misbeliefs are reinforcing the feelings of shame? What wrong conclusions are you making?

Now, *How are you reacting?* Do you tend to move *away* by withdrawing, hiding, silencing yourself, or going quiet? Do you tend to move *toward* by seeking to appease and please others? Or are you more likely to move *against*, trying to gain power over others by being aggressive or shaming back? (You may recognize these as flee, fawn, or fight responses.) Again, keep track of your observations.

3. Now string these two skills together: awareness of your shame and analysis of what's going on. Try to practice "real time" awareness right at the moment you feel shame, and then stop to think about what could be going on for you. It could be something as small as biting your tongue when you really want to defend yourself or snap back at someone who triggered shame in you. Practicing awareness and analysis "in the moment" doesn't have to be done perfectly or take a lot of time out of your day; it just has to be practiced regularly, again and again.

4. The third building block of shame resilience is to reach out to your RB peeps. At first, you might only tell them bits and pieces, and that's okay. You may only tell them after you've had time to process your shame, and you may try to present it to them in a nice, neat, processed package tied with a bow. Be aware of counterfeit vulnerability and be honest with your friends that this is hard, but you want to keep trying.

   You can also practice shame resilience by telling them a very old story of when you felt ashamed—something that happened so long ago, you can now laugh about it. It doesn't matter. Just try to talk about shame. Then try reaching out to your RB peeps in real time, when you're in the midst of the shame tunnel. I promise you, they will help you get out the other side. Empathy is one of the most powerful means to calm our dysregulated brain, so simply having your story listened to with empathy will help you push yourself out to the other side of the shame tunnel.

5. The last building block of shame resilience is speaking your shame out loud. You're already practicing that with the previous building block, but now you'll be saying it beyond your RB peeps and out loud to yourself, to the neighbor, to anyone who will listen. The more often you speak of shame out loud, the more you will become immunized

to it. You also need to accept that shame is a part of life and is here to stay. So, by standing your ground and speaking it, you're facing your shame and refusing to allow it to control you! And you're also getting into the ready habit of asking for help when you need it.

Self-Mastery

I couldn't help but stare, my mouth slightly open, as Byron screamed at my office administrator because she was trying to explain to him why he was being charged for his last "no-show" appointment. To her credit, she remained calm and empathetic but firm that this was office policy, as he had already had one charge waived for another previously missed appointment. He finally noticed me and, looking slightly embarrassed, muttered something under his breath about "unfair policies" before following me into my office.

As he sat down, he began chatting about his week as if the last few minutes had not happened. I let him go on for a few moments before I interrupted him and said, "Byron, what was going on out there?"

I could see him getting defensive and amped up again, as he explained about how unfair our cancellation policies were, since he had a legitimate reason for missing the last appointment due to an urgent business meeting. "I'm just feeling really ripped off right now, and you know money is tight because of my divorce. Honestly, I'm about one step away from taking my business elsewhere."

He paused, and quickly looked at me. "I mean, I'm not saying you're not great and all, Doc, but after the crappy day I just had, this put me over the edge." He then proceeded to list a litany of frustrating things that had happened that day, ending with, "I swear, I think the world is out to get me sometimes."

Byron first started coming to see me because he needed help dealing with the aftermath of his messy divorce. He also needed some strategies to help him manage his stress, because it was becoming intolerable for him. As a business owner—even though he was very successful—he was finding the lack of "staff loyalty" frustrating. It seemed like they were constantly having to replace staff, and he couldn't understand why. He figured it was "young people these days" who just wanted to be pampered and didn't understand a hard day's work.

Part of Byron's business success was due to his charisma and charm, and when he liked you, he was very generous and warm. Funny and boisterous, he was hard not to like—at least initially. But when he felt like you had crossed him, he was quick with his retribution and would cut people out of his circle very quickly. He could also be very demanding as a boss, especially when he was feeling stressed. And when he was upset, everyone knew it. He ruled the company with a firm hand; there was never any doubt as to who was the boss.

But what others didn't know about him was how often he had been bullied as a young boy because he didn't do particularly well in school. He was labeled a "slow learner." His dad also regularly beat him and told him he was stupid, as if that would somehow help him be a better scholar. His mother wasn't much better: she was an alcoholic who spent most of her time locked in her room. Byron ended up dropping out of high school, leaving home, and drifting from one job to another. Yet because he was very shrewd and willing to work hard, he managed to buy into a burgeoning business early on. He rapidly grew that company into a very successful business and became a millionaire before he was thirty.

Byron wore his success well, exuding a bigger-than-life personality and a confidence that was beguiling, persuading others to buy into his ideas and schemes. But underneath that confidence was a deeply insecure man who had a hard time trusting anyone. He managed relationships by being generous—but always with strings attached. He would get angry quickly whenever he felt disrespected, which was often. And when he was hurt, he could be vengeful.

Byron was also known for his short fuse; he figured that was the way to make sure people took him seriously. What he didn't realize was that people found him intimidating and felt like they had to walk on eggshells around him. He didn't know there was an office code the staff would use to alert each other about which Byron was showing up that day, either NiB or NaB—"Nice Byron" or "Nasty Byron."

Inside his blustery self was a hurting young boy who never felt like he was good enough. No matter how much he had proven himself through his business successes, he needed constant affirmation. He loved to brag that his staff was like family to him, and while that meant he would fly them to Las Vegas for a team retreat, it also meant he would be deeply hurt and angry if they failed to appreciate his generosity. I knew it was the hurting boy who was driving Byron's reactivity and manipulations, but unfortunately, that little boy was also a powerful grown man who was used to being the boss, and his behavior was wreaking havoc in his life and with those around him.

At the core of Byron's struggles was that he had never recovered from the trauma of being a victim of others' abuse and cruelty. And so, while it appeared like he was in full control of his life, he subconsciously remained a victim and suffered from an *external locus of control*—meaning that he unconsciously held the belief that the external circumstances and others around him caused his actions, reactions, and suffering. That made him feel very powerless, and so he would rage and cast blame to try to manage his distress.

Additionally, Byron lacked self-awareness of his triggers, and he was completely blind to how others experienced him. He could not see how much of his stress was caused by his own actions and reactions, and how much of others' "rejection" of him was directly linked to how he treated them.

But I knew that before I could teach him any skills to manage his stress and learn to master his own reactions and behavior, I needed to reach that hurting little boy within him. Once Byron experienced healing and grace, he could begin to face the truth of what he needed to change about himself. And then he could understand the good news that he possessed the power to manage his own experience of life and relationships. He just needed to learn the skills of self-mastery.

Defining Self-Mastery

Merriam-Webster defines *self-mastery* as "the ability to control one's own desires and impulses."[1] While that is certainly part of it, there is far more involved in learning to master oneself. I have purposely chosen the word *mastery* in this chapter in part to remind us that, like any skill, it takes lots of practice. Before we dive in, remember: lots of grace, please! Also, as I've been stressing throughout this book, transformation can only come about with repeated implementation of wise choices, so that character development becomes part of our transformed self. We must engage in an intentional commitment to practice our new skills so that we truly become master of ourself.

> **Transformation can only come about with repeated implementation of wise choices.**

While self-mastery is a holistic concept, it is constructed with a number of building blocks. And that's great news; we can master each component and then combine them. I'll outline each one here briefly, and in the Digging Deeper section of this chapter I'll break these down into actionable components you can learn before putting them all together for self-mastery. And just like I said with developing shame resilience, your growth in this area will zig and zag, and self-mastery will be something you will continue to grow in for the rest of your life.

This hard work is worthwhile. You will experience greater joy and true confidence, as well as an expanded capacity to pursue your dreams. Your essential self can fully shine the way you were created to if you're able to mature in these skills. Research results overwhelmingly support the positive effect of developing self-mastery, including better mental and physical health, more positive relations with significant others, greater resilience, and improved ability to cope with stress and life challenges.[2]

Eight Building Blocks of Self-Mastery

1. *Self-awareness* is being conscious of our own thoughts, feelings, behaviors, motivations, and values, knowing our strengths and weaknesses, and, very importantly, understanding our impact on others—what it's like being on the other side of us. No matter how much we'd like to think we are masters of our own universe, we don't operate in a vacuum, and the trajectory of our story will be impacted by the wake of people we leave behind us—for good or ill.

2. *Openness to feedback* means being receptive, welcoming feedback, and having enough self-awareness to sift through feedback and determine what is useful and actionable and what is not. This ties into self-awareness because it's pretty hard to know how other people experience us if we never ask them. We'll stay stuck in an echo chamber of our own beliefs and experiences if we don't allow others' experiences of us into our realm of self-understanding.

This is the biggest trap people who think they have good self-awareness—but really don't—fall into, because they fail to consider how others perceive them. By the way, this isn't about the "truth" of who we are or aren't but rather how our behaviors, actions, and reactions are being interpreted and received by others. We may have great reasons for why we do what we do, but it doesn't matter how pure our motivations are if our actions harm others. And we can't know this if we don't seek objective feedback to develop a more holistic picture of ourself.

3. *Self-efficacy* means feeling responsible for ourself and our life with a can-do, problem-solving attitude rather than a victim or blaming mentality. It includes the ability to initiate and to motivate oneself, rather than waiting for others to do it for us. It also refers to the ability to set realistic goals, problem solve, take action to reach those goals, and remain flexible when circumstances change.

4. *Self-management* is the ability to be highly self-managing of our actions and reactions, rather than being reactive or acting out of habit. It includes the skills to make wise, constructive, and intentional choices as well as the ability to track our responses in real time. This allows us to pause, consider the possible impact of our words and actions, think about what we really want to accomplish, and choose better.

> It doesn't matter how pure our motivations are if our actions harm others.

5. *Emotional maturity* requires the ability to rise above our own personal emotions to understand multiple factors and others' perspectives and see the bigger picture and best response for the situation. It also includes a longer-term perspective than just the immediate situation or our immediate feelings. This perspective doesn't minimize our feelings and needs but takes into account the reality that we are almost always part of a larger situation or group, and our actions/inactions and decisions have an impact that reverberates beyond our own life.

6. *Resilience* is having confidence that life's challenges can be overcome with personal effort, but at the same time requires the ability to discern when situations are out of our control and need to be let go. Resilience also includes the ability to tolerate distress, to face struggle and adversity with tenacity and grit, and to maintain a sense of hope that there is growth through (and because of) the difficult moments of life.

7. *Values-driven perspective* is about making decisions and behaving in a way congruent with our personal values. Cultivating this perspective helps us to know our core values in a conscious,

articulated way but then to also examine whether they are in alignment with *how* we live. Our values always show up unintentionally in what we do with our time, money, and energy, often more than in what we say. We should explore those places to see whether our blind spots may be shielding us from facing this immaturity in our self-mastery. *However*—and this is very key—our personal values don't come at the expense of others or lead to damage or destruction around us. Such a "value" is not in line with true self-mastery; rather it is a fruit of self-indulgence and selfishness.

8. *Commitment to lifelong growth* is a dedication to ongoing self-development and the willingness to take action, practice new skills, and implement those new skills in "real time," even during difficult circumstances. It means not giving up, even when we fail. It means nurturing a growth mindset: we learn to lean into hard experiences, allow failure to be our best teacher, and choose better. And it means cultivating a sense of humor and humility about our foibles and a sense of self-compassion and vulnerability about our areas of growth. Lifelong growth also requires an acceptance of our humanity and the ability to hold with acceptance our beauty and our flaws, even as we continue to grow. (More about this in chapter 15 on the integrated self.)

Internal vs. External Locus of Control

I remember first hearing about the concept of a *locus of control* in grad school and thinking it was just a fancy-dancy term for personal responsibility.[3] While it is that, our locus of control is also more; it underlies a whole host of human struggles and triumphs from the beginning of time. We can even see an example of this happening in the garden of Eden, when Eve first took a bite of the forbidden fruit and Adam followed suit (see Gen. 3:1–13). *It was the snake that made me eat the fruit. It was the woman you gave me who made me eat the fruit.*

Our *locus of control* refers to how much control we perceive we have over our own actions and what happens in our life, as opposed to perceiving events as occurring in our life because of external forces beyond our control. Like most things, this is not a binary, either/or concept but exists along a continuum of *high internal* to *high external*. And even within that spectrum, our locus of control can depend on the day, how stressed we are feeling, and the particular area of our life.

People with a *high internal* locus of control see themselves as having personal control over their behavior, and so they are more likely to take personal responsibility for their actions, which they see as a product of their own agency. They are, therefore, more likely to feel hopeful, less likely to give up when they experience setbacks, more willing to examine what they need to change or how they can solve a given problem, and more likely to have a sense of control over their own destiny and future.

In contrast, individuals with a *high external* locus of control are likely to perceive their behaviors as caused by external forces such as other people, God, or just plain luck (or bad luck). They see events as happening *to* them and struggle with feelings of hopelessness and passivity, low self-esteem, pessimism, an inability to make decisions, and depression. They are also likely to develop *learned helplessness*, which describes what happens when people experience repeated stress or difficulties and so come to believe they're unable to change the situation. As a result, they don't try to improve their circumstances, even when opportunities for change come around. Sadly, individuals with an external locus of control also tend to doubt their own capabilities and attribute their positive outcomes toward luck, fate, or God.

Having an external locus of control can become another way we spiritualize and put all the responsibility for what happens in our life on God. We've got all these wonderfully trite sayings to help us—such as "God is in control," "I'm just waiting on God," "It's all God," or "All things work together for good to those who love God"—to rationalize our inaction and passivity and abdicate our responsibility to do anything to change our circumstances.

Pause and answer the following questions:

Do you have a sense of control about your life and your future? Or would you ascribe it to fate or God?

Do you tend to blame others or the situation if something goes wrong? Or do you tend to examine your own contribution to the situation and think about what you can change?

In what areas of your life do you feel the greatest degree of helplessness?

Getting honest with ourself about how often we lean toward the external end of the locus of control spectrum can help us begin to take mastery over our life. Doing this self-examination puts us in a hopeful place because we can recognize that we *do* have power over our future, and there is much we can do to change our responses and decisions.

Designed to Grow

We've all been designed with an intrinsic motivation toward growth. Look at a young child and notice their sense of wonder and experimentation as they learn how to focus their gaze, grasp an object, turn over, crawl, or walk. How many mistakes or mishaps do they endure in learning the new skill? And notice how they build upon each skill, first learning to walk, then run, then play sports or dance. We have been designed for self-mastery!

Imagine if, the very first time you fell down when you started learning to walk, you threw up your hands and said to yourself, *That's it; this is too hard. I wasn't meant to walk.* Can you hear how irrational this sounds? Yet when we grow into adults, we can lose our motivating sense of wonder, curiosity, and experimentation and our growth mindset.

You have been designed to grow! And that process of growth never stops—frankly, I believe we continue to grow into eternity. If you think about it, if part of our purpose is to know God, and God is so mysterious, unfathomable, and unknowable to our human mind, wouldn't we live in eternity exploring and coming to know more and more of God?

Let's get going! But at the same time, remember, there's no rush. Please don't hurry through each of the exercises below just to get them done. It's not a race, and they're not a tickity-box set of activities. These are lifelong skills you're learning, so keep practicing. Track yourself and name the skills as you notice yourself doing them during the day, and make sure to give yourself a big high five each time (and brag to your friends).

These exercises will definitely take time, so don't worry if you have to do them over an extended period. Just don't forget to do them! Schedule these exercises in your calendar and follow through.

You can do these exercises in order or just pick the ones you most want to work on. It may be helpful to do a quick self-assessment and reread the self-mastery building blocks above to identify which are your strengths, which are areas for growth, and which are big-time weaknesses for you. You can start with your areas of relative strength and just work on improving them, especially if you're feeling particularly sensitive and struggling with some self-doubt. Or, if you feel ready to tackle the area where you need the most work, start with your weakest one.

Keep in mind that you're developing big skills, and the exercises below are simply a way to begin. Starting here is just a way of committing to the lifelong process of developing your self-mastery, so as you grow, it'll be important to look for other ways and opportunities to improve these essential skills.

• • • • • DIGGING DEEPER • • • • •

1. *Self-awareness.* Consider doing a daily examen of your inner world and keep track in a journal so you can start to recognize any patterns.

I use a digital journal so I can do searches and find themes; I can also tag different entries by themes, and search for the entries under these tags.

Ask yourself: *How did I feel today? What was I thinking?* Think about the events of your day and consider what bothered you and what made you feel good. Think about the interactions you had and analyze which ones went well, what was going on, and what made you feel good about them. Then think about interactions that didn't go so well and what was going on. Consider what might have been motivating you. Try to be an objective observer of your day and replay yourself in action and think about what went well, what you could do differently, and what follow-up might need to happen in order to learn.

2. *Openness to feedback.* Now take a deep breath, because seeking feedback isn't for the faint of heart! If you're part of an RB group, start there, but you may also want to choose other people who've observed you in different arenas of your life: work, school, home, church, and so on. Let your selected individuals know that, as part of your growth, you want their regular feedback because you want to build your immunity to the painful feelings of shame, fear, or insecurity whenever you get negative feedback.

Begin to track patterns and understand how your actions/reactions affect those around you. Remember, they are not completely unbiased observers of you, so get feedback from more than a single person and from different realms in your life. Ask them to be as specific as possible. Then, when you get the feedback, sit with it and see what emotions it stirs in you, and whether or not there is a sense of conviction in your soul. Don't be afraid to ask clarifying questions to make sure you understand their feedback, and be as concrete as possible in asking for insight on how and what you need to change.

3. *Self-efficacy.* If, while reading this chapter, you recognized that you tend to be more of an external locus of control person, then this exercise is particularly important for you. Draw a circle and divide it into eight sections (like a pie) on the top half of a sheet of paper and label that circle "Satisfaction/Health." On the outside of the circle, label the eight sections with: physical health, emotional well-being, family relationships, financial health, career/school satisfaction, friendships, partner relationship (even if you're single but want to have a partner), and spiritual health/faith. Then, consider the degree of satisfaction/health you feel you're at in each of these eight areas and color in (from the center of the circle outward) how satisfied/healthy you are in that area. The farther you color from the center, the more satisfied/healthy you feel for that category.

Now draw another similar circle (with the eight pie pieces labeled) on the bottom half of your paper and label it "Self-Efficacy." Go back and reread the definition of self-efficacy, if needed. Then rate yourself on how much agency you feel you have in those eight areas, coloring as above. When you're finished, look at your top circle and highlight the sections in which you have the lowest satisfaction/health; pair them with the sections in your bottom circle that have your lowest levels of self-efficacy. (Can you see how they might be linked?)

Choose one of the slices of those pies to focus on and begin to think through what specific actions you can start taking. If you feel overwhelmed or struggle with follow-through, consider working with a coach who specializes in the area you've chosen (such as a financial coach or physical trainer). You may just need someone or something to help you until you can internalize the discipline needed to continue those action steps on your own. With your coach or on your own, break your growth goal down into baby steps, and then make a commitment to take action. Don't give up!

4. *Self-management.* The first skill to master in self-management is learning to use the *pause*. Each time you feel angry, triggered, or about to leap into action or say something before you think, pause and take five deep breaths. (Use the 4-6-8 breathing technique I mentioned in chapter 6.) If you still feel really upset, choose to walk away from the situation. No good reactions typically come out when you're angry or triggered. Now, this doesn't mean you won't eventually be able to respond in real time in an emotionally mature way (see #5 below), but practice the pause until you have a real handle on your responses. Also consider reflecting on your day, and think about any "do-overs"—situations you wish you had handled differently—and how you *would* handle them if you could do them over. This isn't to beat yourself up but to recognize your patterns. The more you're able to recognize your triggers after the fact, the more you will (eventually) be able to see them happening in real time, stop yourself, and choose better.

5. *Emotional maturity.* Two exercises here will help you with different aspects of emotional maturity. First, do the Play-It-Out Exercise. Mentally play out what could happen if you said or did that thing you wanted to say or do. Think about how others in the conversation or situation might react. Play it forward in your mind and consider what the outcome might be. Will anyone be hurt? Will there be any unintended consequences? Will you have to go back and repair the relationship or situation? Take it as far as you can imagine. Don't worry about being silly; this is just about teaching your brain to think ahead.

The second exercise is the Mirror Exercise. For this one, you're going to need a partner. As you're having a conversation, try to put yourself in their shoes and consider what they may be feeling and thinking. Your job here is simply to try to understand their perspective and experiences, not to put forward your own. Try to reflect their thoughts back to them, saying something like, "So what I think I'm hearing you say is . . ." This is especially valuable if you're in a disagreement with someone. Pause from arguing your perspective and just seek to understand. This doesn't mean you agree with them; it simply allows you to step back from your own thoughts and feelings to understand another person's.

6. *Resilience*. Building resilience requires reflection. Continue to reflect on your family of origin and some of the trauma, misbeliefs, and negative narratives you might have. Try to be honest about your level of personal resilience—your ability to face difficult things, including emotional pain and shame. Reflect also on your tolerance of uncomfortable things, especially related to your personal growth. Are there situations or people you've been avoiding? Consider which of the earlier chapters you were tempted to skim because they stirred up a lot of strong reactions. If you're able to be honest with yourself about your resilience, then you'll also be able to acknowledge where you need help. (There are forms of therapy that help you build your resilience in tolerating distress, or you may need trauma therapy.)

It may be time to deal with the parts of your story that have held you back from flourishing. It may also be time to recognize you may be immature in some areas of your resilience because of your family background (for example, you experienced a fearful, overprotective family system), because you've spent a lifetime avoiding, or because you're in a codependent relationship with an over-functioner who has protected you from facing your fragility. Remember, if you're struggling with this level of self-reflection, you can do a very brave thing and go back to your trusted friend/family group and ask for feedback on where they see you as resilient and where they see you as fragile. Don't beat yourself up! (That's a surefire way to remain stuck.) Resilience is like a muscle that can be developed; you can start taking baby steps to strengthen this.

7. *Values-driven perspective.* Most of us kind of "know" our values but haven't really taken the time to articulate them or identify our top nonnegotiables. There are some great free values exercises available online; I'm including one here that is offered by Brené Brown.[4] While she suggests you pick your top two values, I would encourage you to start broader and try identifying your top fifteen values (see her values list for ideas). First list them in order of general priority, but then categorize them further into "nonnegotiable," "important to have," and "nice to have." Then try to filter your decisions, particularly major ones, through your top six values. Think through your life right now—your job, your relationships, your church, your ministries, etc.—and consider how they line up with your top six values. Does anything need to change? This doesn't mean quitting a job or a relationship, but it does mean being intentional about what shifts you have to make, however small, to begin to move toward alignment with your values.

You may also find you're feeling tension because your values are competing with each other, and that tension is keeping you stuck, so make sure you're very clear which of your values is more important to you and why. For example, you may be staying in a job that drains you (a likely sign that it's not reflective of one of your core values) but the stable income and benefits it provides are helping you care for your family, which is a top value for you. If you choose to stay in a situation that doesn't fully align with your core values, recognize that other core values are motivating your choice, and you're not trapped or without the ability to choose. Knowing you have agency can be freeing.

Begin to pay attention to any tension you feel in your soul, because it may mean you've been living in a way that's out of line with your top values.

8. *Commitment to lifelong growth.* Be honest with yourself: How much of your time, energy, and thought go toward personal growth? This should be evident through things like the kinds of books you read, the YouTube videos you watch, or the podcasts you follow. But remember, insight isn't enough. If you're a "wisdom gatherer," but you're not applying what you're learning to your own life, then you may be suffering from counterfeit-growth-itis. True growth requires an investment of time and energy, and if you jump from book to book or podcast to podcast but never really "work the program" deeply on any one developmental area, then you're doing the tickity-box approach to personal growth, not authentic transformation. Instead, be reflective about what concrete steps you have taken to grow, as well as changes you've noticed in yourself, and ask for feedback from people who've walked with you long enough to notice those changes. Then make plans for your next step. Make this an annual or semiannual process—a "personal retreat" time when you reflect on your areas of growth and plan your next steps for the coming season.

True Connection

Jared's face was beaming in a way I'd never seen before. He was almost giddy as he told me about how he'd proposed to his girlfriend while they were at a park the previous weekend. Completely unsuspecting, she had at first resisted his attempts to go down a particular path. But she finally agreed when he convinced her that the view down that way was spectacular. As they walked down the pathway, they noticed some mysterious lights in the distance. When they finally got close, she saw it was multiple LED candles stuck into the ground in the shape of a heart, surrounding a blanket scattered with red roses. There was also a picnic basket, a bottle of champagne, and two champagne glasses. He even had a string quartet waiting for them that started to play Celine Dion's "The Power of Love" as soon as they rounded the corner.

Jared couldn't stop laughing as he talked about how cheesy his proposal was, because he and his girlfriend had a running joke about how much she hated that kind of thing, and she had playfully warned him against ever doing anything like that. But when the moment came, she punched him lightly in the chest and then fell into his arms, laughing and crying. And as he got on his knee and proposed to her, she jumped up and down with excitement.

Tears began running down his cheeks as Jared told me about how happy he was, how deeply in love he was with his fiancée, and how grateful he was for the work he and I had done to open his heart up to the possibility of love. I couldn't help but weep with happiness for him too, as he talked with such a sense of hope for his future.

It was hard to imagine the sullen Jared who'd first walked into my office—forced to come because of his boss—being the same man who was now overcome with joy. It had not been an easy journey for him. He'd had to face not only his deepest wounds and hurts from his past but also take ownership for his own actions that had pushed people away. He also had to choose to open up his heart and trust, which had been terrifying to him.

But with his hard work and commitment to his healing journey, Jared had become a much more effective and beloved leader; he was less stressed and obsessed with work (which paradoxically led to even better results, as he learned to lean on his team to help); he had repaired his relationship with his parents; and he had finally begun to develop true friendships and started dating. He now saw that every bit of the pain he'd endured to get to where he was today was so very worth it. It was his willingness to risk his heart and his ability to be vulnerable with his girlfriend that brought him to this point: he was just about to marry the love of his life.

Healthy Connections as Fruit of Our Transformation

Jared's choice to risk his heart was not easy, because human relationships hurt. They hurt a lot. And when the hurt comes, it's natural to blame others or feel that we're somehow flawed and unlovable. It's human to resist trusting others in the face of relational pain or to withdraw into isolation to protect our broken heart. But the despair of being truly alone—of choosing protection over connection—will kill our soul. Being disconnected from others was not the way we were meant to be. Ever.

Brené Brown puts it this way:

A deep sense of love and belonging is an irreducible human need from the moment we're born until the day we die. We are biologically, cognitively, physically, and spiritually wired to love, to be loved, and to belong. When those needs are not met, we don't function as we were meant to. We break. We fall apart. We numb. We ache. We hurt others. We get sick. There are certainly other causes of illness, numbing, and hurt, but the absence of love and belonging will always lead to suffering.[1]

Let me personalize this for you. You have picked up this book and are reading it for a reason. Perhaps it was the title that intrigued you, or a friend recommended it, or maybe your partner bought it for you and put it on the night table as a not-so-subtle hint that this book might be good for you.

You may not be reading this book because you *felt* your need for connection but because you just wanted to work on improving yourself. And that is wonderful!

But I have to warn you: with personal transformation comes self-honesty and a capacity to feel our human longings and hurt even more. We become ever so tender to our need for love and belonging. As painful as that is, if you're feeling this way, it's great news. Because the fruit of your personal transformation *will be* healthier connections. Oh, it's not like abracadabra, you wake up one morning and have all these amazing connections magically in place. It's far more subtle than that. Working on yourself gradually shifts the day-to-day normalcy of your life, which ultimately transforms the trajectory of your life and your relationships.

> **Being disconnected from others was not the way we were meant to be. Ever.**

Each step you take in your personal growth makes you braver, more vulnerable, more self-honest, and more self-aware. And that, in turn, awakens you to your need for healthy connections, which opens you up to more courage, more risk, more vulnerability. This cycle absolutely will transform your relationships—the ones you currently have and the ones yet to come. Listen again to Brown: "We cultivate love when we allow our most vulnerable and powerful selves to be deeply seen and known, and when we honor the spiritual connection that grows from the offering of trust, respect, kindness, and affection."[2]

You'll also grow in your wisdom to discern who your true-blue peeps are—and who might not be in the place you need them to be. No matter how much you may long for it, don't waste energy wishing someone to be where you want them to be, as it's not in your hands to make that happen. Even as you can only love others as much as you love yourself, so it is the same for the people in your life. Yes, it will hurt you when they choose not to do the work to become one of your trusted safe people—and not just because of your own longings for true, intimate connection with them but also because you love them so much that you long for the same transformation for them. You have seen the light, and you deeply desire it for them too.

But living out of your integrated self means letting go of the need to fix others and accepting that they are where they are (more on this in the next chapter). In the meantime, *you* get on with the business of your own transformation and pursuit of healthy connections with safe people. As Brown reminds us, "Love is not something we give or get; it is something that we nurture and grow, a connection that can only be cultivated between two people when it exists within each one of them—we can only love as much as we love ourselves."[3]

As you focus on your own personal transformation, it *will* change your relationships. And your changed relationships will impact your community. Which will change the world.

It's Time to Step Out

I hope you see the importance of healthy connections with others. I've probably pressed in on this need more than anything else because healthy relationships are so core to our design, and I really want us to *get* this. If we are to live as our God-given essential self, healthy and intimate connections to others and to God have to be nonnegotiable. Science, the Bible, psychologists, pastors—everyone agrees we're wired for relationship.

As you grow your relationships, remember to have patience and grace for yourself, as many of us struggle in intimate relationships because of those attachment wounds we talked about in chapter 7. And even as I outline some ideas on how you can work on your relationships (see below), I don't want to make light of the work that can be required to heal from those wounds. Be prepared: even as you move forward in building healthier connections with others, during times of stress—particularly relational stress—your attachment wounds may be triggered, and unhealthy, self-protective behaviors can recur. When they do, consider them as signs that your soul is distressed and your attachment longings need care. Remember, your shadow self comes out when you feel exposed, shamed, insecure, scared, or hurt, so practice self-compassion and self-soothing.

If you are a Jesus-follower, go to him as your ultimate source of love and empathy. And if it is your relationship *with him* that is your trigger, still go to him. It will be a step of faith to do so, but it is only through your courage to risk going to Jesus that you'll experience healing in your relationship with him. Like all other broken relationships, healing will take time, persistence, courage, and vulnerability. So be patient with the process and don't give up.

If you're finding yourself constantly triggered and having difficulties breaking free from the fear dance in your relationships, I strongly recommend you consider therapy, because it often takes a consistent relationship with someone who can remain grounded and nonreactive, is in your corner, and is skilled at helping you process your trauma. Your partner or close friend, while they can be part of your healing journey, typically cannot bear the weight of your pain.

Aside from feeling helpless in the face of your pain, they also have their own stories and trauma that can be inadvertently triggered by you, which can keep you both locked into a dance of mutual pain.

Our Attachment Style

It is not uncommon for us to be attracted to someone whose attachment style is the very kind that will trigger our anxieties! It is therefore important for you to understand your own attachment style, as well as that of your partner or a friend with whom you have a close relationship.

Attachment theory was first developed by John Bowlby and Mary Ainsworth in the late twentieth century, and there have been many studies since then that demonstrate the robustness of that theory.[4] Put briefly, our attachment style is our mind's way of gauging how safe we feel in a relationship. We do not consciously choose our style; it is formed based on the degree of attunement, connection, security, and safety we felt with our parents or primary caregivers. As a result, we are most likely to see our attachment style play out in adulthood in our intimate relationships, which require trust, vulnerability, and safety to be healthy.

Out of Ainsworth and Bowlby's work, four basic attachment styles have been posited, although individuals can also have a blend of styles. As I outline them, think about which one(s) you resonate with most. This is a very important first step to understanding your particular relational style, and why you may react the way you do to attachment ruptures.

The first style is *secure attachment*. Those with this style grew up with attuned parents who gave them consistent care and love, and so as adults they tend to feel confident and open to pursuing intimacy. They can connect to others while maintaining their own sense of autonomy. In relationship, those with a secure attachment style tend to be emotionally available to their partner, emotionally grounded, and nonreactive. Now, this doesn't mean these people never get triggered, but if they're in a relationship with someone who is also securely attached, those relational ruptures happen infrequently and are often repaired quite quickly. Some questions to ask yourself to see if this is your style are:

Do I find it easy to be affectionate with my partner or people I love?

Can I express my needs and wants to my partner or close friends?

When I have an argument with my partner or close friend, do I still feel confident about our relationship?

Am I able to express my opinion comfortably when I disagree with someone?

The second style is *anxious attachment*, which describes people who have an almost constant need for connection and reassurance from their partner or close friends because of their underlying fear of abandonment. They tend to put the people they love on a pedestal and can be preoccupied with the relationship, fearful of losing it or being left alone. Others may experience them as "clingy" and hypersensitive, but at the same time, when triggered, these people can be reactive and even aggressive and suspicious, even when there is no reason to suspect their partner or friend of disloyalty. Some questions to consider are:

Do I often worry that my partner or close friend will stop loving me?

Do I fear that when someone gets to know the real me, they won't like who I am?

Do I tend to get quickly attached in a relationship and then spend a lot of time thinking about it?

Am I very sensitive to my partner's or friend's mood?

The third style is *avoidant attachment*, and it describes people who can *seem* warm and capable of connection but are often emotionally distant or very independent in intimate relation-ships. Others may experience them as noncommittal, and even if they do commit to a relationship, these people can tend to put up walls, be emotionally private, and avoid emotional intimacy. They struggle to be vulnerable with others and can seem satisfied with rather superficial connections with others. See if these questions resonate with you:

> Do I find it difficult to emotionally support my partner or close friends when they are feeling down?
>
> Do I tend not to share my innermost thoughts and feelings with my partner or close friends?
>
> Is my independence so important to me that I prefer not to involve my partner or my friends in my decisions?

The final style is an *ambivalent attachment* (also called *anxious-avoidant*) and refers to those who tend to blow hot and cold in their intimate relationships and have significant difficulties in romantic relationships. While they may seem initially capable of connection, they struggle with their self-worth and often feel betrayed and see their partners in a very negative light when they feel triggered. Relationships tend to be filled with unpredictability and chaos, which mirrors their fear-based and chaotic inner world and the conflict they feel between a desire to attach and a deep fear of at-tachment. People with this attachment style can come from abusive or traumatic backgrounds. Consider these questions:

> Do I tend to jump from partner to partner or friend to friend, as I find I am easily disappointed or feel betrayed?
>
> Do my relationships tend to be like a roller coaster, filled with highs and lows and lots of drama?
>
> Do I struggle to be consistent in how I feel about my partner or friends?
>
> Can I be demanding of my relationships but then "disap-pear" on my friends or partner?

While it's important to understand your attachment style—and that of your partner and close friends—the good news is that you *can* change your attachment style if it's not a secure one. The exercises in the Digging Deeper section below are a great place to start on this healing journey. There is so much you can do in your personal growth to shift into healthier connections with others. As I'm sure you're starting to see—as with all other areas of personal growth and transformation—it's about first developing insight, then making changes in your actions and reactions, and finally practicing your new skills and responses until they become part of your norm.

· · · · · · DIGGING DEEPER · · · · · ·

1. Spend some time considering your attachment style, as well as that of your partner and close friends. Look at some of your recent conflicts in light of this insight and spend some time journaling. Think about when you've been triggered and what has happened to cause that reaction in you. For example, it may be, "I feel irritable when my friend gets clingy," or "I feel anxious when my partner is quiet and withdrawn." Identify your reaction as well as the action/inaction on the part of your loved one that triggered your feelings. Then consider how some of *your* actions/inactions could be triggering your loved one's reactions. We are never in a vacuum in relationships, as we tend to co-trigger each other!

2. Look for themes to the triggers and consider what might be your underlying wounds and unmet needs. Trace these themes to some early childhood experiences, and journal how these patterns may be manifesting in your current or prior relationships. If you're a person of faith, spend some time in prayer with the ultimate Healer, and let yourself be as raw and transparent as you can be. Feel free to be angry

with God, unfiltered. For me, it took several seasons of journaling with God before I was able to see my patterns clearly. But that time with God was rich and meaningful, and I now know experientially—to the depth of my being—how loved I am and how secure I am in my relationship with him. And from that place of security, I have been able to risk being more honest and vulnerable with my husband and close friends, leading to even more healing and growth in my core relationships.

3. Practice being open in expressing your hurt feelings to your loved ones—particularly the more vulnerable emotions of hurt, shame, and fear. If your most immediate emotion is anger, spend some time processing your anger to unearth the underlying hurt. The hurt is there, as anger is a secondary emotion that protects us from our more vulnerable underlying emotions, so continue processing and journaling until you gain insight. If this is too difficult for you, then you may need the help of a therapist. If you communicate with your loved one in anger, you will shut the door to healthy communication and shared understanding, even if your anger is legitimate. Also, if the trigger is particularly strong and you are feeling very emotional, it's wise to spend some time on your own processing rather than unload all those intense feelings on your partner. Wait until you're calm enough to be clear in expressing how you're feeling and what you need from your loved one.

When communicating your vulnerable emotions, use "I" statements rather than "you" statements, which can come across as blaming and critical. For example, you may say, "I feel hurt when you look at your phone when I'm talking to you. I would appreciate it if you would focus on me when we're talking, as I feel more connected with you." The more you and your loved one understand and attend to each other's needs in a caring, responsive way, the closer you will feel, and the more confident you will be of your capacity to repair when conflict inevitably occurs.

Sometimes our loved ones don't respond in healthy ways and may even purposely provoke our wounds, if they are very angry or hurting themselves. Even well-intentioned people will unconsciously revert to old habits and can trigger an old wound, even after discussion. If that's the case, it's important to restate your needs, and if they're still disregarded, it's essential to have clear boundaries and hold them. Talking about how to set and hold boundaries is beyond the scope of this book, but Cloud and Townsend's book *Boundaries* is an excellent resource.[5]

4. Assess your personal relationships and categorize them into three groups. Keep in mind that these categories can be fluid, and people can be A in some areas but B in other areas of your life, and they can also move around.

   A group: those few relationships that are truly reciprocal, and people with whom you can be safe to be your vulnerable self. These people are teachable, take ownership for their part of the dance, and are working on their own growth. You feel valued by them, and vice versa. Your core values are in alignment, and you expect and receive mutual care from each other.

   B group: the bulk of the people in your life. They can be very positive and enjoyable relationships, but you don't have expectations of meeting each other's needs, and they also don't have the power to really hurt you.

   C group: the people in your life where the giving only goes one way—as in you to them. You have no expectations of them, but you care and serve them. They are not taking much ownership for their own growth, and so you let go of any expectations of change. Sadly, this may include your partner, child, parent, or family member. In that case, they remain in your life, but you set very clear boundaries concerning your time and energy, and what you will/will not tolerate from them.

5. For people of faith, your relationship with God can also suffer from attachment injuries because of how your parents or church may have modeled him for you. If you're finding it difficult to make the leap from your head to your heart in your connection with God, please make it a priority to work on healing this very important relationship. Consider working with a spiritual director who has the skill, insight, and discernment to help you on this very important and tender part of your soul's healing. Wholeness in the core of who you are cannot occur fully without healing your attachment to God.

The Integrated Self

I stared in disbelief at the results. *Low in integration? Surely there's been a mistake. Come on, I'm a psychologist who teaches this stuff! I do personal growth for a living! I must've skipped a line or two on the questionnaire, and somehow it messed it all up for me. Stupid test!*

I'd taken an online test that rated my level of integration, and I knew the results were all wrong. I didn't care that they claimed to have 95 percent accuracy on their results. My defiant denial was rearing its ugly head. I was not ready to get pushed out of my happy place. My very accurate sense of self reassured me that it was obviously a flaw in the design of the test, and my shadow self patted me on the back, affirming how mature and healthy I really was.

The report went on to indicate that I struggled to see my blind spots and tended to get "stuck" in the strategies I used to deal with stress. Also, I had a slight tendency to distort reality toward "faking good." (What the heck?)

To my eternal embarrassment, I sent an email to the test designer and questioned my results. I told them I wanted to understand the statistics behind the findings—but really, I wanted to pinpoint where it went wrong. "I am very healthy!" I wanted to yell at them, but of course I was far too mature to do so other than in my head.

I must admit, it took me a while to get past the *ouch!* of those results. I sometimes still mutter about it to myself and anyone who will listen. It's not easy to look into a mirror and see the truth about ourself. But that is part of the work of integration: looking at the good *and* the bad in ourself and holding them both with acceptance and compassion.

Integration

The root meaning of the word *integration* is to "make whole." Interestingly, the root word for *healing* is the German word *heilen*, which also means—Guess what?—to "make whole."[1] Even more specifically, *heilen* means to bring together *all* the parts to make something whole. Not holding one part over the others, not hiding one part because we don't like it, and not pretending that a missing piece isn't, in fact, missing. It's bringing together all the parts and accepting that they all constitute the whole.

But we often mistake healing or wholeness to mean "perfection," without pain or suffering. And so, we spend oodles of time, money, and energy trying to perfect ourself and our life and to remove pain and suffering from our experiences.

And I wonder if maybe we're missing the point.

I often ask people if they think Jesus was perfect. Of course, they always say yes, but then I'll remind them he had body odor, bad breath, and constipation. I'll also remind them he had big emotions and experienced fear, pain, and suffering. And died an excruciating death.

Yes, he overcame death, was resurrected, and is seated at God's right hand in the heavenlies. But we can't minimize the importance of seeing what happened *before* all that good news. If we skip past the kind of life Jesus lived on earth, we skip past the life we're meant to live.

Holistic living—the kind of life Jesus lived—means holding our human frailties, suffering, and weaknesses together with our resilience, joy, and strengths. It's living with acceptance and compassion but also with the determination to pursue *goodness* in the life we live. To do better. Jesus was *perfectly good*, and even so, he had to mature from an infant to an adult. He made his share of mistakes as he was maturing (I'm sure his mom thought he was a goofball at times), and as he grew in wisdom and stature, he learned from those mistakes.

Holistic living also includes holding together what seems contrary as part of the complexity of human experiences. Experiencing great despair doesn't detract from our capacity for joy. Experiencing the heights of joy doesn't diminish our times of unbelievable pain. If we want to live like Jesus lived, we do it with compassion, grace, integrity, humility, vulnerability, and goodness. With *humanity*.

> **If we skip past the kind of life Jesus lived on earth, we skip past the life we're meant to live.**

And we keep growing and transforming to be better and better versions of ourself. We cannot become our true, essential self if we deny our darkness and our pain, if we repress aspects of ourself that we deem to be "unacceptable," or if we are unaware of the impulses that underlie our decisions, actions, and reactions. And we cannot live an integrated life if we cannot accept that there will always be unfinished business and unanswered questions this side of heaven. We must let go of our need for certainty and black-and-white answers to all of life and surrender to the Mystery of life—the Creator of life—who will always be beyond our comprehension.

I've been asked if I regret the decisions I've made in my life. But that's a difficult one for me to answer, because I've grown so much through the messiness of my mistakes and misjudgments. I'm a much better version of myself now because of the lessons learned through the hardship and pain I've experienced, even when—perhaps especially when—that pain has come through my own decisions and choices.

I've learned through these hard lessons to be able to carry together what may seem incompatible: darkness and light, suffering and hope, my shadow self and my essential self. I've learned to honor my story and my pain, to be compassionate to the tender parts of my heart, to recognize that my triggers come from a place of deep hurt, and yet to know that I'm strong and resilient and my faith will get me through. I can honor my story and pain yet choose not to be reactive or allow that pain to limit me or keep me in a place of self-protection and fear. I can accept the reality of our broken world and the systemic change that needs to happen without being trapped in bitterness, nonproductive anger, blame, and a victim mentality.

Essential me doesn't mean perfect me. We can take everything that's bright and beautiful in us and introduce it to our shadow side. We can let our altruism meet our egocentrism, our generosity meet our scarcity, our courage meet our cowardice, our joy meet our grief.

Integrated Living

As I mentioned in the introduction, I believe we have a God-given "soul-ish" self. Jesus exhorts us in Mark 12:30, "Love the Lord your God with all your *heart* and with all your *soul* and with all your *mind* and with all your *strength*" (emphasis mine). He seems to differentiate the soul as some essential part of us *apart* from our heart, mind, or body (strength). But—and this is critical to understanding integrated living—he also mentions the heart, mind, and body as equally *part of us*.

In our intellectual knowledge and expertise–focused Western world, we seem to value the mind over everything else, and we forget we are also heart and body. Science now shows us that we have neurons, or neural pathways, not just in our brain but also in our body (gut) and in our heart.[2] These neural pathways gather information that helps us make wise decisions; understand ourself, others, and the world around us; and live healthier lives. That means our emotions and our gut feelings are also sources of intelligence, just like the thoughts going on in our head.

Integrated living, therefore, means we take into account the information from all three centers of intelligence in our life. It means we don't value one over the others but seek a balanced perspective. To be an integrated self is to be unified in our thoughts (mind), emotions (heart), actions (body), and identity (soul). Because of how beautifully God designed us, those parts of us are always gathering information; it's just that we can lose touch with one or more aspects of ourself and then experience a lack of wholeness, a lack of health. Integration requires growing in our awareness of our thoughts, feelings, and actions, and being able to find cohesion between all three.

When we are living out of sync with our centers of intelligence and are unaware we are doing so, we are also unaware of our *blind spots*. We don't know what we don't know. As much as I wanted to believe I was high in integration, those test results showed me something I needed to face about myself: I tend to value my feelings over logic (I'm hearing my husband saying, "Amen!"), and I can sometimes ignore (sigh) an objective view of the facts. As a people pleaser, I can also ignore what my body is telling me: that someone is taking advantage of me and I'm about to be running on empty.

Because I'm highly skilled at eliciting positive feedback from others and getting great results, it was easy for me to deny that my shadow self—motivated by a need to perform and be perfect to gain the positive regard of others—was in full operation. Because those strategies work!

Until they don't.

And when that happens, I stay stuck. I don't grow. I still have the same reactions and actions.

Integrated living means we are highly self-aware, able to gather intel from all sources in real time, and can stop our old reactions and choose better. It means a high degree of fluidity to change our responses to suit the situation—not to further our personal gain but for the betterment of others and the world, to fulfill our purposes in this world. And over time, as we practice integrated living, those new skills become part of our habitual responses. We are transformed to be like Jesus—in our unique way—just as we're designed to be. We live out of our God given essential self and shine his glory in a personalized way that changes the world.

DIGGING DEEPER

1. Think of a recent situation that was stressful, filled with conflict, or otherwise difficult for you to handle. What were you thinking? Feeling? How did you respond? What were your underlying motivations for your actions? Where and how did your shadow self show up? What strategies did you use to cope or to handle the situation? Were these strategies familiar ones? How would you handle things differently, in retrospect? Try to answer these questions without judgment, simply as an objective, curious observer of yourself. Seek feedback if you can, again with a stance of curious open-mindedness.

2. After all the processing you've been doing as you've read this book, where do you think you might have blind spots? (Hint: think about your fears, insecurities, shame, and unmet needs.) Where do you tend to rationalize your reactions/actions? Again, feedback from trusted people can help with this!

3. Rate yourself on your degree of fluidity in responding to stressful situations. This isn't about your temperament (some of us are more flexible than others) but rather your ability to sense when you're triggered, stop your old response, and respond differently. Think of a successful time you were able to do that, then think about another situation that didn't go so well.

4. Remember that living as your integrated self requires insight and self-honesty, but it also requires a tolerance for

ambiguity, complexity, and mystery. Pay attention to when you feel tension within yourself, as often it can mean there is a lack of resolution to the situation. Try to let go of the need to control the outcome or have the answer or solution, and allow yourself to develop tolerance for living in the unknown and unfinished.

5. Which of the three intelligences do you tend to pay most attention to (mind, heart, or body)? Which do you pay least attention to? For the next week, be intentional about paying attention to your weakest source of intelligence. You might even ask someone you know who's strong in that center for some strategies, or simply watch them and see what they do differently from you.

Becoming Our Essential Self

In thinking about what to write for this concluding chapter, I was really tempted to write, "See all of the above. The end."

You may feel like you've hung in there and slogged through all the exercises to get to the end of the book—where surely you would find your essential self waiting.

But you know I'm not about the tickity-box activities. (Bingo, you're transformed!) I know, I know . . . I wish personal growth was like a smarmy fiction story with a clichéd happy ending. I don't know how many times I've whined to my friends about how hard this personal growth thing is, and when can we get to the ending, already? But real life isn't like a manufactured story arc with a definitive resolution. (Although I find that all great fiction books that really move me purposely leave unanswered questions, unfinished story lines, and messy characters with unresolved stuff . . . much like real life.)

We need to recognize and remember that becoming our God-given essential self is a constant process.

So while I can't give you a nice, neat ending all wrapped up with a pretty bow, I do want to conclude with a hopeful and aspirational reflection, to celebrate how far you've come, and to remind you that there *is* a God-given essential *you* who is starting to come out of hiding. You—in all your beautiful, wonderful, intentional design—are a treasure, worthy of unearthing. *You* are a reflection of God's glory in your own unique way, and this world needs you to show up as the true, authentic, essential *you*!

> Real life isn't like a manufactured story arc with a definitive resolution.

Pursuing your essential self needs to be something *you* do for yourself, with God's guidance. To that end, I have a soul-ish activity for you to end with, which will be different from some of the other practical exercises offered in previous chapters. I'd like to encourage you to write a life manifesto to celebrate and put into writing all that you've done through the course of this book and will continue to do in your journey of transformation.

Encyclopedia Britannica defines *manifesto* as "a document publicly declaring the position or program of its issuer. A manifesto advances a set of ideas, opinions, or views, but it can also lay out a plan of action. . . . Manifestos often mark the adoption of a new vision."[1]

Many manifestos evolve over time, and I suspect most go through several iterations before going public. Give yourself time to capture what you want your life vision to be—but start putting some thoughts down in writing *now*; don't delay, or else it will never get done (you know that's true). Go back over your Digging Deeper exercises and pull insights from there. It doesn't have to be perfect; you just have to get started. Give yourself permission to edit as much as you want. In fact, I would encourage you to review your manifesto annually, to make sure it still captures your vision.

If you're a person of faith, I would also encourage you to sit in prayer with God and invite him into this process. He knows who he's created you to be, so who better to involve? You can choose to do your manifesto in words, in pictures or song, through a craft or other creation, or some combination of any of that. Regardless of how you do it, your life manifesto ought to inspire you, remind you, humble you, and draw you back to your truest, essential self.

I'm purposely keeping this open-ended, as this is not a set of activities for you to go through. If you find articulating a manifesto difficult and want clearer steps or instructions, don't worry. You can add *that* into your manifesto—the fact that you don't like doing this and feel uncomfortable doing it, but are still doing it. And that, my friend, is worth celebrating.

I'm ending with the life manifesto I first wrote years ago and have since edited several times to give you an example and hopefully also to inspire you. Before you read it, I want to pause to thank you for following along with me and for believing in yourself and this process enough to commit your time to reading this book and working on your growth.

I am filled with so much awe and wonder, and I can't wait for you to see how incredible you are. I am so excited for your life and for the purposes you will fulfill living as your God-given essential self!

My Life Manifesto

Today, I choose freedom.
The freedom that has been promised to me by Jesus,
because his truth *has* set me free.
I choose freedom from people-pleasing, perfectionism,
    and performance.

Today, I choose to come out of hiding.
Because Jesus sees me for who I am.
And loves me for who I am.
Therefore, I choose authenticity and honesty.
I choose to take responsibility for my voice—
my opinions, feelings, and choices.

Today, I choose to live the full life.
The full life that has been promised to me by Jesus,
who came to bring me life to the full.
I choose:
courage instead of fear
leaning into instead of withdrawing
self-awareness instead of denial
conviction instead of shame
forgiveness instead of bitterness
humility instead of pride
vulnerability instead of hiddenness
self-acceptance instead of self-rejection
connection instead of isolation.

Today, I choose to believe God's truths—
that I am beloved, chosen, treasured, holy, and blameless.
I choose to come against the lies of the enemy, the thief of
    my soul—
I come against the lies:
that I am only loved for what I do and not for who I am
that I should be ashamed of who I am
that I am unlovable and unacceptable
that I am nobody special
that it's all up to me
that no one is there for me.

I come against the fears of:
abandonment
rejection
anger/conflict
aloneness.

Today, I choose to surrender myself to God,
the One who is sovereign, loving, and good.
The One who created me in love and with delight.
The One who designed me intentionally as my essential self.
The One who created me for a purpose.
The One who gave me the precious gift
of reflecting a beautiful aspect of his incredible,
    illuminous, unbelievable glory.

Today, I choose to remember that God is with me and for me.
Today, I choose to rest in him,
center myself in him,
draw strength and wisdom from him.
Today, I choose gratitude.
Today, I choose to savor his good gifts.
Today, I choose to pursue growth and transformation and
    to trust that this is his will for my life.
Today, I choose to let go of the protection of my shadow self
    to live out of the freedom and beauty of my God-given
        essential self.

Acknowledgments

I am still marveling at the gift of writing this book!

They say it takes a village, and I would not argue with that. I can't even begin to name all the people who have been a part of my journey, culminating in this book. But there are a special few who need mentioning.

First of all, my agent extraordinaire, Don Pape, who believed in me from the very beginning and would not give up on the book he knew needed birthing in me. He has been my encourager, cheerleader, and advocate. Thank you, my friend. We will sit down together one day over Tim Horton's coffee and Canadian butter tarts!

And then there's Rachel Freire O'Connor, my incredibly gifted editor, whose gentle spirit and sensitivity to my soul allowed me to shine as my essential self. She chose to take a chance on a Taiwanese Canadian woman without much of a platform, simply because she felt like I had something worth saying. And through her insightful editing and discerning guidance, she has turned this book into the gem it is today. Thank you for helping to bring out my voice, Rachel. And thank you, also, to the wonderful team at Baker Books, for the support and counsel you provided throughout the entire publishing process. You seriously rock!

And lastly, I would not be the person I am today if it weren't for my precious hubby, Peter; my beloved progeny, Amanda and Cameron; and my dearest friends. *You are my people.* You have seen the best and the worst in me and have continued to love me, believe in me, challenge me, speak truth to me, and be that safe place I need to show up as my essential self. My journey of growth—and all that has been captured in this book—could not have happened without you. I love you all so much and thank you from the bottom of my heart.

Notes

Introduction

1. Parker J. Palmer, *On the Brink of Everything: Grace, Gravity, and Getting Old* (Oakland, CA: Berrett-Koehler Publishers, 2018), 6.

2. Mishal Reja, "Trump's 'Chinese Virus' Tweet Helped Lead to Rise in Racist Anti-Asian Twitter Content: Study," ABC News, March 18, 2021, https://abc news.go.com/Health/trumps-chinese-virus-tweet-helped-lead-rise-racist/story ?id=76530148.

3. Bong Joon Ho and Han Jin Won, "Parasite: Outstanding Original Screenplay," accessed November 14, 2023, https://deadline.com/wp-content/uploads /2020/01/parasite-script.pdf, 113.

4. Craig S. Keener and John H. Walton, eds., *NRSV Cultural Backgrounds Study Bible: Bringing to Life the Ancient World of Scripture* (Grand Rapids: Zondervan, 2019), 68.

5. Keener and Walton, eds., *NRSV Cultural Backgrounds Study Bible*, 256.

Chapter 1 Our Stone Age Brains

1. National Human Genome Research Institute, "Genetics vs. Genomics Fact Sheet," September 7, 2018, https://www.genome.gov/about-genomics/fact-sheets /Genetics-vs-Genomics.

2. The Chimpanzee Sequencing and Analysis Consortium, "Initial Sequence of the Chimpanzee Genome and Comparison with the Human Genome," *Nature* 437 (September 2005): 69–87.

3. P. Sah, E. S. L. Faber, M. Lopez de Armentia, and J. Power, "The Amygdaloid Complex: Anatomy and Physiology," *Physiological Reviews* 83, no. 3 (July 2003): 803–34.

4. Timothy D. Johnston and Laura Edwards, "Genes, Interactions, and the Development of Behavior," *Psychology Review* 109, no. 1 (2002): 26–34.

5. "Three Basic Instincts and 27 Enneagram Subtypes," Integrative Enneagram Solutions, accessed October 10, 2023, https://www.integrative9.com/enneagram /27-subtypes/.

6. Marie Levorsen et al., "The Self-Concept Is Represented in the Medial Prefrontal Cortex in Terms of Self-Importance," *The Journal of Neuroscience* 43, no. 20 (May 2023): 3675–86.

7. Katherine Wu, "Love, Actually: The Science behind Lust, Attraction and Companionship," *Science in the News* (blog), February 14, 2017, https://sitn.hms.harvard .edu/flash/2017/love-actually-science-behind-lust-attraction-companionship/.

8. Ralph Adolphs, "The Social Brain: Neural Basis of Social Knowledge," *Annual Review of Psychology* 60 (January 2009): 693–716.

9. Mario Garcés and Lucila Finkel, "Emotional Theory of Rationality," *Frontiers in Integrative Neuroscience* 13 (April 2019): 1–24.

10. Amrisha Vaish, Tobias Grossmann, and Amanda Woodward, "Not All Emotions Are Created Equal: The Negativity Bias in Social-Emotional Development," *Psychological Bulletin* 134, no. 3 (May 2008): 383–403.

11. M. Ena Inesi, "Power and Loss Aversion," *Organizational Behavior and Human Decision Processes* 112, no. 1 (May 2010): 58–69.

12. Amos Tversky and Daniel Kahneman, "Advances in Prospect Theory: Cumulative Representation of Uncertainty," *Journal of Risk and Uncertainty* 5 (October 1992): 297–323.

13. Marion Sonnenmoser, "Friend or Foe?," *Scientific American Mind* 16, no. 1 (April 2005): 78–81.

14. Ida Esther Berger, Peggy Cunningham, and Minette E. Drumwright, "Identity, Identification, and Relationship through Social Alliances," *Journal of the Academy of Marketing Science* 34, no. 2 (March 2006): 128–37.

15. Rob Nelson, "Competition," Untamed Science, October 2013, https:// untamedscience.com/biology/ecology/competition/.

Chapter 2 Nature, Meet Nurture

1. William G. Iacono and Matt McGue, "Minnesota Twin Family Study," *Twin Research* 5, no. 5 (October 2002): 482–87.

2. R. A. Power and M. Pluess, "Heritability Estimates of the Big Five Personality Traits Based on Common Genetic Variants," *Translational Psychiatry* 5, no. 7 (July 2015): 1–4.

3. Jack P. Shonkoff and Deborah A. Phillips, eds., *From Neurons to Neighborhoods: The Science of Early Childhood Development* (Washington, DC: National Academies Press, 2000).

Chapter 3 In the Grip of Fear

1. Fushun Wang et al., "Editorial: Neurotransmitters and Emotions, Volume II," *Frontiers in Psychology* 13 (May 2022): 1–3.

2. Lucas S. LaFreniere and Michelle G. Newman, "Exposing Worry's Deceit: Percentage of Untrue Worries in Generalized Anxiety Disorder Treatment," *Behavior Therapy* 51, no. 3 (May 2020): 413–23.

Chapter 4 Shame on You!

1. *Merriam-Webster*, s.v. "joy," accessed September 11, 2023, https://www .merriam-webster.com/dictionary/joy.

2. Patricia A. DeYoung, *Understanding and Treating Chronic Shame: Healing Right Brain Relational Trauma* (New York: Routledge, 2022).

3. John A. Sturgeon and Alex J. Zautra, "Social Pain and Physical Pain: Shared Paths to Resilience," *Pain Management* 6, no. 1 (January 2016): 63–74.

Chapter 5 Behold, Our Shadow Self

1. Mary Ainsworth and John Bowlby, "An Ethological Approach to Personality Development," *American Psychologist* 46, no. 4 (1991): 331–41.

2. "Developmental Sciences at UMass Boston," YouTube video, 8:33, uploaded by UMass Boston, March 12, 2010, https://youtu.be/vmE3NfB_HhE.

3. Mathew A. Harris, Caroline E. Brett, Wendy Johnson, and Ian J. Deary, "Personality Stability from Age 14 to Age 77 Years," *Psychology and Aging* 31, no. 8 (December 2016): 862–74.

4. Tasha Eurich, *Insight: The Surprising Truth about How Others See Us, How We See Ourselves, and Why the Answers Matter More than We Think* (New York: Crown Publishing, 2018).

5. These descriptions of motivations and underlying fears are adapted from "Introducing the Enneagram as a Personality Type Model: What Is the Enneagram and the iEQ9 Enneagram Test?," Integrative Enneagram Solutions, accessed October 10, 2023, https://www.integrative9.com/enneagram/.

Chapter 6 The Gift of Self-Compassion

1. Kristin Neff, "Research," Self-Compassion: Dr. Kristin Neff, accessed October 10, 2023, https://self-compassion.org/the-research/.

2. Kristin D. Neff, "Self-Compassion: Theory, Method, Research, and Intervention," *Annual Review of Psychology* 74 (2023): 194–95.

3. Neff, "Self-Compassion," 196.

4. Neff, "Self-Compassion," 204–5.

5. Neff, "Self-Compassion," 200–201.

6. Neff, "Self-Compassion," 205.

7. Kristin Neff, "Self-Compassion Guided Practices and Exercises," Self-Compassion: Dr. Kristin Neff, accessed October 10, 2023, https://self-compassion.org/category/exercises/.

Chapter 7 Trust Issues

1. "Learn about Bowen Theory," The Bowen Center for the Study of the Family, accessed October 10, 2023, https://www.thebowencenter.org/core-concepts -diagrams.

2. American Psychiatric Association, *Diagnostic and Statistical Manual of Mental Disorders*, 5th ed. (Arlington: American Psychiatric Publishing, 2013), 271–72.

3. Erin K. Morris, Cara Laney, Daniel M. Bernstein, and Elizabeth F. Loftus, "Susceptibility to Memory Distortion: How Do We Decide It Has Occurred?," *American Journal of Psychology* 119, no. 2 (Summer 2006): 255–74.

Chapter 8 The Stories We Tell Ourself

1. Fernando Blanco, "Cognitive Bias," in J. Vonk and T. Shackelford, eds., *Encyclopedia of Animal Cognition and Behavior* (New York: Springer, 2017), 1–7.

2. J. Ehrlinger, W. O. Readinger, and B. Kim, "Decision-Making and Cognitive Biases," in Howard S. Friedman, ed., *Encyclopedia of Mental Health*, 2nd ed. (Waltham, MA: Academic Press, 2016), 5–12.

3. Rachel A. Gordon, Robert Crosnoe, and Xue Wang, "Physical Attractiveness and the Accumulation of Social and Human Capital in Adolescence and Young Adulthood: Assets and Distractions," *Monogram of Social Research in Child Development* 78, no. 6 (December 2013): 1–137.

4. Brené Brown, *Daring Greatly: How the Courage to Be Vulnerable Transforms the Way We Live, Love, Parent, and Lead* (New York: Avery, 2012), 228.

5. Mark Van Ryzin, Diana Fishbein, and Anthony Biglan, "The Promise of Prevention Science for Addressing Intergenerational Poverty," *Psychology, Public Policy, and Law* 24, no. 1 (February 2018): 128–43.

6. Stephanie Madon, Lee Jussim, and Jacquelynne Eccles, "In Search of the Powerful Self-Fulfilling Prophecy," *Journal of Personality and Social Psychology* 72, no. 4 (1997): 791–809.

7. Robert Rosenthal, "Self-Fulfilling Prophecy," in Vilayanur Ramachandran, ed., *Encyclopedia of Human Behavior*, 2nd ed. (San Diego: Academic Press, 2012), 328–35.

8. Benjamin Gardner, Phillippa Lally, and Jane Wardle, "Making Health Habitual: The Psychology of 'Habit Formation' and General Practice," *British Journal of General Practice* 62, no. 605 (December 2012): 664–66.

Chapter 9 Fake It Until You Make It

1. Cody Hiatt, Brett Laursen, Karen S. Mooney, and Kenneth H. Rubin, "Forms of Friendship: A Person-Centered Assessment of the Quality, Stability, and Outcomes of Different Types of Adolescent Friends," *Personality and Individual Differences* 77 (April 2015): 149–55.

2. *APA Dictionary of Psychology*, s.v. "self-esteem," accessed October 10, 2023, https://dictionary.apa.org/self-esteem.

3. *APA Dictionary of Psychology*, s.v. "self-acceptance," accessed October 10, 2023, https://dictionary.apa.org/self-acceptance.

4. University of Hertfordshire, "Self-Acceptance Could Be the Key to a Happier Life, Yet It's the Happy Habit Many People Practice the Least," Science Daily, March 7, 2014, https://www.sciencedaily.com/releases/2014/03/140307111016.htm.

5. Douglas L. MacInnes, "Self-Esteem and Self-Acceptance: An Examination into Their Relationship and Their Effect on Psychological Health," *Journal of Mental Health and Psychiatric Nursing* 13, no. 5 (November 2006): 483–89; Marcus A. Rodriguez, Wei Xu, Xiaoming Wang, and Xinghua Lui, "Self-Acceptance

Mediates the Relationship between Mindfulness and Perceived Stress," *Psychological Reports* 116, no. 2 (April 2015): 513–22; Journal of Consumer Research, Inc., "Admitting Our Faults: When Does Self-Acceptance Trump Self-Destruction?," Science Daily, May 21, 2014, https://www.sciencedaily.com/releases/2014/05/140521133308.htm; Juliana G. Breines and Serena Chen, "Self-Compassion Increases Self-Improvement Motivation," *Personality and Social Psychology Bulletin* 38, no. 9 (May 2012): 1120–32.

Chapter 11 The Strength of Vulnerability

1. Brené Brown, *The Gifts of Imperfection*, 10th an. ed. (New York: Random House, 2020), 19.

2. Brown, *Daring Greatly*, 1.

3. Brown, *Daring Greatly*, 2, emphasis mine.

4. Brown, *Daring Greatly*, 117–21.

5. Brown, *Daring Greatly*, 37.

6. Mark A. Lumley et al., "Emotional Awareness and Other Emotional Processes: Implications for the Assessment and Treatment of Chronic Pain," *Pain Management* 11, no. 3 (May 2021): 325–32.

7. Michael Cronquist Christensen, Hongye Ren, and Andrea Fagiolini, "Emotional Blunting in Patients with Depression, Part I: Clinical Characteristics," *Annals of General Psychiatry* 21, no. 1 (April 2022): 10.

8. Michael Cronquist Christensen, Hongye Ren, and Andrea Fagiolini, "Emotional Blunting in Patients with Depression, Part II: Relationship with Functioning, Well-Being and Quality of Life," *Annals of General Psychiatry* 21, no. 1 (June 2022): 20.

9. David Fetherstonhaugh, Paul Slovic, Stephen M. Johnson, and James Friedrich, "Insensitivity to the Value of Human Life: A Study of Psychophysical Numbing," *Journal of Risk and Uncertainty* 14 (1997): 283–300.

10. Afsoon Eftekhari, Lori A. Zoellner, and Shree A. Vigil, "Patterns of Emotion Regulation and Psychopathology," *Anxiety Stress Coping* 22, no. 5 (October 2009): 571–86.

Chapter 12 Shame Resilience

1. Simon Dein, "Against the Stream: Religion and Mental Health—The Case for the Inclusion of Religion and Spirituality into Psychiatric Care," *BJPsych Bulletin* 42, no. 2 (May 2018): 127–29.

2. Christine J. Park, "Chronic Shame: A Perspective Integrating Religion and Spirituality," *Journal of Religion and Spirituality in Social Work: Social Thought* 35, no. 4 (September 2016): 354–76.

3. David V. Alvarez, "Using Shame Resilience to Decrease Depressive Symptoms in an Adult Intensive Outpatient Population," *Perspectives in Psychiatric Care* 56, no. 2 (April 2020): 363–70.

4. Brené Brown, "Shame Resilience Theory: A Grounded Theory Study on Women and Shame," *Families in Society: The Journal of Contemporary Human Services* 87, no. 1 (January 2006): 43–52.

5. K. J. Van Vliet, "Shame and Resilience in Adulthood: A Grounded Theory Study," *Journal of Counseling Psychology* 55, no. 2 (2008): 233–45.

6. Tara Ryan-DeDominicis, "A Case Study Using Shame Resilience Theory: Walking Each Other Home," *Clinical Social Work Journal* 49, no. 3 (2021): 405–15.

7. Virginia Rondero Hernandez and Carmen T. Mendoza, "Shame Resilience: A Strategy for Empowering Women in Treatment for Substance Abuse," *Journal of Social Work Practice in the Addictions* 11, no. 4 (2011): 375–93.

8. Brown, *Daring Greatly*, 75.

Chapter 13 Self-Mastery

1. *Merriam-Webster*, s.v. "self-mastery," accessed September 11, 2023, https://www.merriam-webster.com/dictionary/self-mastery.

2. Chiara Filipponi, Peter J. Schulz, and Serena Petrocchi, "Effects of Self-Mastery on Adolescent and Parental Mental Health through the Mediation of Coping Ability Applying Dyadic Analysis," *Behavioral Science* 10, no. 12 (November 2020): 182.

3. For more information, see Amanda O'Bryan, "Internal vs External Locus of Control: 7 Examples and Theories," Positive Psychology, August 17, 2021, https://positivepsychology.com/internal-external-locus-of-control/.

4. Brené Brown, "Living Into Our Values," Brené Brown, accessed October 10, 2023, https://brenebrown.com/resources/living-into-our-values/.

Chapter 14 True Connection

1. Brown, *Gifts of Imperfection*, 34.

2. Brown, *Gifts of Imperfection*, 35.

3. Brown, *Gifts of Imperfection*, 35.

4. Ainsworth and Bowlby, "An Ethological Approach to Personality Development," 331–41.

5. Henry Cloud and John Townsend, *Boundaries: When to Say Yes, How to Say No to Take Control of Your Life*, updated and expanded ed. (Grand Rapids: Zondervan, 2017).

Chapter 15 The Integrated Self

1. Merriam-Webster, s.v. "healing," accessed November 12, 2023, https://www.merriam-webster.com/dictionary/healing.

2. Julius Kuhl, Markus Quirin, and Sander L. Koole, "Being Someone: The Integrated Self as a Neuropsychological System," *Social and Personality Psychology Compass* 9, no. 3 (March 2015): 115–32.

Chapter 16 Becoming Our Essential Self

1. *Britannica*, s.v. "manifesto," accessed July 17, 2023, https://www.britannica.com/topic/manifesto.

Dr. Merry C. Lin is a psychologist, podcaster, and speaker with over thirty years of clinical expertise. She is the executive director of Dr. Lin & Associates, where she leads a team of psychotherapists, life coaches, and leadership experts. In her consulting work, Dr. Merry provides expertise in a wide variety of areas, including mental health, stress management, personal growth, leadership, and team development. In her clinical practice, she provides psychoeducational and diagnostic assessments for people of all ages to identify learning differences, neurodiversity, and behavioral/emotional/mental health issues.

Dr. Merry is also an advocate for social justice and works globally to equip and support leaders who serve human trafficking and abuse survivors. As part of her advocacy work, she works to build awareness of mental health and diversity and to help equip families and communities to create safer spaces for those who are on the margins.

A wise counselor and respected speaker, Dr. Merry can be heard on her popular podcast, *The Fully Lived Life*, as well as on several TV and media shows where she is a regular guest. She is married with two adult children, and she is actively involved in her community. She loves adventure and travel, and there aren't too many exotic foods she won't try! When relaxing, she can be found curled up with a good book or spending time with her family and close friends.

CONNECT WITH DR. MERRY

DrMerry.com
Personal Website

DrLinAndAssociates.com
Practice Website

TheFullyLived.Life
Podcast

@DrMerryLin

@DrMerryLin

@MerryCLin